TENKARA
TODAY

TENKARA
TODAY

MORGAN LYLE

STACKPOLE
BOOKS

Guilford, Connecticut

To my wife, Susan Epstein,
and the great relief of having her to talk to.

STACKPOLE BOOKS

Published by Stackpole Books
An imprint of The Rowman & Littlefield Publishing Group, Inc.
4501 Forbes Blvd., Ste. 200
Lanham, MD 20706
www.rowman.com

Distributed by NATIONAL BOOK NETWORK
800-462-6420

Copyright © 2019 Morgan Lyle

Photography by the author unless otherwise noted.

British Library Cataloguing in Publication Information available

Library of Congress Cataloging-in-Publication Data available

ISBN 978-0-8117-3782-1 (paperback)
ISBN 978-0-8117-6766-8 (e-book)

♾™ The paper used in this publication meets the minimum requirements of American National Standard for Information Sciences—Permanence of Paper for Printed Library Materials, ANSI/NISO Z39.48-1992.

Contents

Acknowledgments

I am grateful to the many people who helped me write this book, especially Daniel Galhardo and Christopher Stewart, who patiently re-answered questions I had already asked them many times over the years, and who also shared photos. My thanks to all those who gave generously of their time for fishing trips and telephone interviews, and who also took or provided photos, including: George Daniel; Tom Sadler; Adam Klagsbrun; Ed and Judy Van Put; Tom Rosenbauer; ERiK Ostrander, John Vetterli, and Rob Worthing; Dennis Kim; Jeff Dannaldson; Matt Sment; Go Ishii; Phillip Werner; Joe McDonough; Brian and Colby Trow; Anthony Naples; Robb Chunco; and most especially my wife, Sue Epstein, for the many wonderful photos she took, and for the love and support she so freely gave.

Introduction

I like tenkara fishing because of what it is, not because of what it is not.

What it is not, of course, is fishing with a rod and reel. In tenkara fishing, the angler uses only a rod, with the fishing line attached directly to the rod tip. There's no reel involved.

Why no reel? Because the old-time Japanese mountain men who caught trout to sell and to eat didn't bother with them. Tenkara is the modern recreational form of that kind of fishing.

The *shokuryoshi*, as the commercial trout fishers were known, didn't bother with reels because reels weren't necessary. You don't need to cast very far when fishing a rushing mountain stream, and you don't need to reel in the fish you catch—you can just lean the rod back behind you, take the line in your hand and pull the fish to your feet. There may be some trout you can't reach, and a few may get away before you can scoop them up in your net, but for the most part, fixed-line fishing is a very effective way to catch trout.

The *shokuryoshi* weren't fishing for fun. One would hope they enjoyed their work, but their fishing was their business, and a reel would have been an expense and a complication that contributed nothing to the bottom line.

Japanese recreational anglers in the second half of the twentieth century had as much access to reels as their counterparts in the rest of the developed world. But those anglers who developed tenkara as a recreational pursuit maintained the fixed-line tradition. For them, the appeal of tenkara was the rushing mountain stream itself, and the mountains that gave rise to it, and the pretty fish that live in

Tenkara fishing evolved in Japan as an effective method for catching trout in swift mountain streams. SUSAN EPSTEIN

ix

it. They could have done their mountain stream fishing with fly rods, as many of their countrymen did, but they preferred to use tenkara rods. Tenkara was its own thing.

When Tenkara USA introduced fixed-line trout fishing to the American fishing public in 2009, the company emphasized simplicity. A pricey reel, a long line, a huge selection of trout flies, and the gadgetry of modern fly fishing were not necessary for successful, enjoyable trout fishing, any more than they were necessary for the *shokuryoshi.*

By 2009, I had been fly-fishing for twenty-five years, and I liked it just fine. I did not wish I didn't have to use a reel. A nice fly reel is a thing of beauty. I enjoy holding and looking at and using them. I enjoy making nice, long casts. I take pleasure in understanding the many kinds of flies, how to make them, and when to use them. I do not think of fly fishing

as unnecessarily complicated. On the contrary, the complexity is part of the fun.

I was not yearning for a simpler kind of fishing when tenkara came along. Tenkara won me over because of what it was, not what it wasn't.

Tenkara rods are cool, sleek, and smart. They flex delightfully when casting. It is easy to make very precise casts, and to control the line in order to present the fly to the fish in a natural way. I love how the rod telescopes down to less than two feet long, so you can shove it into a day pack and take it with you when you go for a hike or a bike ride. And for a sport that claims to be simple, tenkara has plenty of fun gear to fiddle with—different kinds of lines, special spools to keep them on, and flies, including flies that look different from the ones in the American fishing magazines.

Best of all, having to fish without a reel and a long line gives me a new set of fun little

This wild rainbow trout leaped three times after being hooked on Esopus Creek in New York. After it was finished leaping, it was efficiently landed on a Tenkara Bum rod, photographed, and released. MORGAN LYLE

problems to solve. I have to get close enough to the fish to reach it with my short line, usually by wading in its stream. And once the fish is hooked, I have to "play" it until it gives up the fight without being able to allow it to race away, pulling line off a reel, or to winch it to my feet.

While I liked my fly-fishing stuff, I did enjoy the simplicity of tenkara. Attaching a line and extending a tenkara rod was quicker than uncasing and assembling a fly rod, attaching a reel, and pulling the line through the rod's guides. Deciding not to bother trying to "match" the myriad tiny insects trout eat and just fish with an old-fashioned, half-inch fly was liberating. Carrying less stuff made me feel lighter on my feet when I fished. I appreciated the way tenkara anglers treated small fish with affection and respect. Naturally, I appreciated how little tenkara costs compared to fly fishing. And as an old punk rocker, I was drawn to tenkara's willingness to buck the establishment.

Lots of fly fishers weren't drawn to tenkara at all. "Where I'm from that's how we fished when Mom wouldn't buy us a rod and reel," wrote one guy, one of the more polite guys, in a mostly tenkara-bashing Facebook thread. "I was ahead of this trend!"

But there are other examples of hunters and anglers choosing to use less technology in their pursuit of game. In this book, you'll read Japanese tenkara expert Go Ishii say using tenkara instead of a rod and reel is like shooting a pistol instead of a rifle. I think it's more like hunting with a bow instead of a gun. Bow hunting requires more stealth, because you have to be much closer to your quarry to be successful, and a different set of skills. The Fish & Wildlife Service once did a survey in which they asked bow hunters why they preferred bow hunting

to using a rifle, and by far the top response was for the challenge.

Some people prefer to ride bicycles with no gears—and even no brakes—just for the experience. "It's the intimate connection between rider and bike, as difficult to articulate as the pleasure of driving a car with a manual transmission instead of an automatic, but just as real," wrote cyclist Neil Bezdek on Bicycling .com. Some people prefer to take photographs with a fixed lens, instead of a zoom lens. They often make you work harder to get the shot you want, but they also make beautiful images.

I talk a lot in this book about how tenkara is a very effective way to catch trout, and it's true. I catch a lot more trout with tenkara gear than I do with fly-fishing tackle. But there is no denying that tenkara restricts your options. You can't cast as far as you can with a fly rod or a spinning rod. And some fish are just too big to be landed with some rods. But every kind of recreational fishing is better at some things than others. Tenkara is a tool whose purpose is to throw a virtually weightless lure into a stream where a trout will see it, then land that trout when it bites. It does those things well. And the direct-connected line and the willowy nature of the rod result in a more intimate connection with a captured fish than any other tackle I've used.

It was very interesting to see a fully formed hobby imported to the United States from another culture. To Western fly fishers, tenkara was familiar and foreign at the same time. We wondered whether it was a fad that would fizzle out in a couple of years, or a substantial new category of fly fishing. Neither of those proved correct. Thousands of tenkara rods have been sold in the US by small but well-established businesses, and newbies continue to take it up. Ten

years on, it's hard to see it as a fad. But most of the big-name fly rod companies have shown zero interest in making tenkara rods, and tenkara hasn't risen much above the level of a curiosity over in the accessories department of the fly-fishing retail world.

So tenkara is, instead, its own thing. It can be seen as a variety of fly fishing, or as an alternative. It can be an added activity on your bike-packing trip, a fun way to kill a couple hours at the bluegill pond, or a full-on obsession involving travel and high-end gear. It has an exotic and modern feel, and it's been fun these last ten years figuring out how to play a game where the rules are in a foreign language. I hope you enjoy reading about it, and I hope you'll consider trying tenkara yourself.

Tenkara was designed for catching trout in swift, cold streams. GEORGE DANIEL

CHAPTER 1

A Different Kind of Fly Fishing

In 2009, I had a great gig: I got to write a column about fly fishing every week for the sports section of the *Daily Gazette* newspaper in Schenectady, New York. By that time, I had been obsessed with fly fishing for more than twenty years, and getting paid to write about it was great fun. Even so, finding a newsworthy story each and every week could be a challenge, so I always kept an eye out for anything new and unusual. One day I learned about something called tenkara. It was unusual, to say the least.

After all, it was universally agreed that having a long line wound onto a reel was an indispensable part of fishing. How in the world could you catch fish with no reel at all, just a short line attached to the tip of a rod?

I soon found out that tenkara fishing is an exceptionally effective way to catch trout and other kinds of fish. It's also inexpensive, compared to Western-style fly fishing, and easy to learn. It's the way people caught fish with artificial flies for at least seventeen centuries, before reels came into common use. And while this kind of fishing gear severely limits how far you can cast, it also greatly improves your ability to fish the water you can reach.

Tenkara was exported from Japan to the Western world in April 2009. Over the next few years, it attracted a following, comprised of both veteran fly fishers like me and people who had never fished at all. Tenkara became a subculture of American fly fishing. Some anglers put their reeled fly rods in the closet and became tenkara purists. Some even traveled to Japan to learn from the masters.

Tenkara isn't only for small streams. This trout was caught on the wide Housatonic River in Connecticut. JOE MCDONOUGH

Over the next decade, an American tenkara tackle industry emerged. Today, it is easy to get a whole outfit—rod, line, tippet, and flies—for a couple hundred bucks, plus the waders you'll need to walk around comfortably in cold, stony streams.

This is how you use it.

The trout stream lies before you, glittering and chattering in the afternoon sun. It's three or four feet deep at most, but full of rocks, currents, and tiny waterfalls where a trout can hide from birds of prey while snatching aquatic insects that drift by in the eternal current. The small stretch of stream directly before you holds dozens of places to drift a fly.

The fly itself may be as simple as a small chicken feather wound onto a hook so that its fibers splay out like the wriggling legs of a mayfly, with a little sewing thread wrapped onto the hook shank to suggest the fly's slender abdomen. Your tenkara rod is telescopic,

Tenkara flies, like the Keeper Kebari, are simple but effective. SUSAN EPSTEIN

and when collapsed it's less than 2 feet long. You remove the little cap from its tip to reveal a short length of braided nylon with a simple knot tied near its tip. From your small gear bag, you take your coiled line and attach the rod end to the braided nylon (known as a lillian) with a simple knot. To the other end of the line is tied a tippet—a few feet of thin, clear fishing line—and your fly is tied to that.

Line attached, you extend your rod, pulling out the spaghetti-thin tip section, followed by successively thicker segments, until the rod reaches its full 12-foot length—ridiculously long by Western fly-fishing standards, but also ridiculously light, three ounces or less. You step into the shallow water at the edge of the stream, looking behind you for room among the streamside trees and bushes for your backcast, then looking at the stream for the troutiest-looking spot you can reach from your casting position. A quick rearward flick of your wrist tosses the line into the air behind you, and a forward flick sends line and fly out over the water. The fly drops as gently as a feather (since that's mostly what it is) into the water just upstream of a protruding rock, slips beneath the surface, and drifts with the current past the rock and alongside the small eddy behind it.

You hold your rod at an angle above the stream. The line hangs down to the water at a similar angle, and you watch the line as your fly is carried along in the mysterious underwater world. Your cast goes untouched, so you try again, in case there was a trout there that didn't notice the first time. This time, the fly's downstream progress is interrupted, and almost as soon as you become aware of that, you feel a strange weight at the end of the line, and then the panicky energy of a hooked fish.

The tenkara stance: ready to strike the moment a trout takes the fly. SUSAN EPSTEIN

The remarkably flexible rod bends deeply, even when fighting a small trout. That flex is the key to your victory. The trout can try to dash away, but is always pulled back by the big, soft spring. The fish may pull back hard and shake its head, it may zigzag a little, but in fairly short order you'll be able to hold the rod behind you and pull the trout to your feet, where you scoop it from the water. Now, you either admire your fish for a few seconds, slip the barbless hook out of its jaw and let it swim away, or you bonk it on the head and put it in your creel for a dinner of stream-fresh fish.

An Intuitive Way to Fish

In April 2017, I walked through the Brooklyn neighborhood where I live to fish in the lake in Prospect Park. I carried a tenkara rod (well, technically a *keiryu* rod, but it works the same way—more on that in the chapter on rods), collapsed down to its closed length of 22 inches. Over my shoulder I carried a small satchel with a couple boxes of flies, a few tenkara lines, a few spools of extra tippet and some small, simple tools like nippers to cut line, and a hemostat to easily remove a hook from a fish.

The Prospect Park lake holds largemouth bass, crappie, bluegill, and a few carp. I worked my way along the shoreline, picking spots where overhanging trees wouldn't affect my ability to cast the long rod (it can be fished at either 12 or 14½ feet), and caught and released a couple of decent crappies and a small bluegill. It was a sunny late afternoon with as much people-watching as fishing.

Tenkara fishing is trout fishing, but tenkara gear can be used for many other species, such as bluegill.
MORGAN LYLE

At one point, as I stood along the water's edge, three teenage guys, one on foot, one on a bike, and one on a skateboard, all carrying light spinning rods, passed behind me on the blacktop path. The one on the skateboard made an audacious request: "Sir, do you mind if I try that?"

Besides making me feel old ("sir"?), his request gave me pause. The tip of a tenkara rod is easily broken if you're not careful. But this guy's genuine curiosity was immediately apparent. I decided to trust him and handed him the rod.

Here is the point of the story: It took him about three casts to figure out how to toss the line behind him and then fling it out over the water, dropping the fly right where he wanted, near the shoreline bushes. The fact that he was already interested in fishing surely helped, and he also seemed like one of those graceful people who get the hang of physical things quickly. Still, three casts—no classes, no lessons. Tenkara is that intuitive.

My new friend caught no fish during his short experiment; there probably weren't any in this particular spot or he would have gotten at least a curiosity nibble. Had we been on a trout stream with a decent population of fish, I bet he would have landed one in five minutes or less.

Fly fishers have always taken a certain amount of pride in having mastered something tricky. Learning to fling 40 feet of PVC fly line around takes some doing. Tenkara fly fishing, on the other hand, really isn't tricky. I'll explain how it's done, but most people seem to figure out on their own how to toss a fly where they think there might be a fish. One of the narratives you used to hear when tenkara first arrived in the United States was "minutes to learn, a lifetime to master." There are subtle advanced techniques for those inclined to master them, but I pretty much settled for the "learn" part and I've been catching fish ever since. Sure, my accuracy has improved with practice. But most of the time I'm only dimly aware of what my casting arm is doing. The casting almost happens by itself. My attention is focused on the water, on where I want my fly to land, and what I want it to do once it gets there.

This ease of use made tenkara popular right way with some outdoorsy types whose priority is not fishing, but who often find themselves near really nice places to fish. Through-hikers, mountain bikers, car campers, even ounce-counting ultra-light backcountry trekkers suddenly had access to a very capable fishing system that added barely any weight or bulk to their packs.

Tenkara rods pack down to less than 2 feet long, so they're great for hiking and backpacking. Philip Werner, author of SectionHiker.com, always has a tenkara rod in his pack. PHILIP WERNER

Hike for the afternoon, stop and fish a mountain stream for a while, and secure some fresh-caught trout for dinner at your campsite.

Philip Werner, author of the SectionHiker.com website, is an example.

A mid-fifties Boston resident who "up and quit" his job in the software industry to launch the website, which is named after the intrepid trekkers who hike sections of the two thousand-mile Appalachian Trail, Werner is out of doors "every day," he said. "Even if it's just a five-mile hike. I go backpacking about once a week, mostly one- or two-night trips."

Werner bought a tenkara rod five years ago, and began using it regularly a couple of years later. Today, he rarely leaves home without it.

"I never fished before tenkara and was always put off by the gear and techniques required to fly-fish with a rod and reel," he said. "I took a lesson with a guide who gave me my first and only tenkara lesson and now do both, although I primarily do tenkara. Actually it's gotten to the point where I carry a tenkara rod on every hike I take and usually use it every day, tying flies at night."

Those folks, however, are probably the minority. I think most people who have taken up tenkara are primarily interested in fishing. Some are fascinated by tenkara's exotic nature and its Japanese philosophical underpinnings. Some enjoy how its credo of simplicity runs counter to the clutter of our gadgety modern world. Some just love the sleek sexiness of the rods.

Tenkara's simplicity and the light weight of the tackle make it especially attractive to children.
GEORGE AND AMIDEA DANIEL

None of this would be enough if the gear didn't perform, of course. We go fishing to catch fish. Make no mistake: Tenkara is an excellent way to fish, especially for trout in streams. If it wasn't, people wouldn't have used this gear to feed their families back in the day.

The ease of use has also led some to look at tenkara as a kind of fly fishing lite, a stage of learning on the way to "real" fly fishing. (I've noticed this theme from companies that carry some tenkara gear but are primarily interested in selling "real" fly rods and reels.) I couldn't disagree more. Tenkara is a complete method of fishing; it's not a stepping-stone to anything. Like I said, I fished with a rod and reel for a long time before I ever heard of tenkara, and I still do when the situation calls for it (like saltwater fly fishing) or when I just happen to feel like some Western-style fly casting. But if I'm going trout fishing, especially on a stream with lots of "pocketwater"—rocks, eddies, currents, plunge pools—I will use a tenkara rod because I will catch more fish than I would with a rod and reel.

Let me try to answer a few common questions about tenkara.

IS TENKARA FLY FISHING?

In a sense, the answer is "obviously," since you're fishing with a fly. Tenkara casting also is very similar to Western-style fly casting. But let's back up a little and discuss what fly fishing is and how it differs from "regular" fishing with a rod meant to throw bait or lures.

In every kind of fishing except fly fishing, the angler throws a lure or a baited hook to the place he or she thinks there is, or will soon be, a fish. In fly fishing, what you actually throw is the line itself.

The term fly fishing comes from the fact that the lures we call "flies" are meant to suggest the things trout eat the most—aquatic insects, such as mayflies, caddisflies, and stoneflies. These artificial flies are almost weightless. They amount to little more than a feather tied on a lightweight hook. You can't throw them. "How far could you throw a feather?" asked famed author and fly-fishing teacher Joan Salvato Wulff.

So instead, you fling the fly line, which is a thin, supple cord of PVC-coated nylon. The leader, a short length of clear line attached to the end of the line, and the fly, tied to the end of the leader, are carried out over the water with the line.

That's what you do in tenkara fishing, too, and that is why I have always said tenkara fishing is without question a form of fly fishing.

IS TENKARA MORE EFFECTIVE THAN WESTERN-STYLE FLY FISHING?

In some situations, yes.

Let's begin by acknowledging tenkara's obvious limitation: You can't cast very far. A typical tenkara rod is around 12 feet long, and the line attached to its tip, including the tippet, is usually 12 to 16 feet. That's a maximum of 30 feet of range—if the rod and line are both horizontal. Most of the time they're not; the rod angles up and the line angles back down. So your fishing range is usually around 20 feet.

Many who have spent years mastering Western-style fly casting would be embarrassed to make a 20-foot cast. A classic Western fly-fishing situation involves a trout feeding regularly at the surface of the stream, picking off floating mayflies, 30, 40, even 60 feet away, and successfully reaching that fish is a significant part of the game.

Wisconsin's Driftless region is laced with trout streams that are perfect for tenkara fishing. Badger Tenkara founder Matt Sment casts upstream in a tasty pool. ANTHONY NAPLES

The tenkara angler either wades closer to the fish or, if that's not possible, looks for another one within reach. New tenkara anglers are often surprised by how many fish are within 20 feet of where they stand. There are more fish around the shore of a lake than in its middle. And in a trout stream, if there's no good "holding" water right in front of you, you can usually wade the stream to a better place to cast. A typical tenkara rod gives you all the distance you need to reach a lot of fish.

In Western fly fishing, most of the casting line in that 30-, 40-, or 60-foot cast is floating on the surface of the water. Sometimes, this is no problem. But in many cases, the current pulls the line, dragging the fly away from where the fish is feeding.

With a tenkara rod, in most cases, you have no line lying on the water at all. Your line angles down from your rod tip, with only your fly and a foot or two of clear "tippet" in the water. It's very easy to get your fly to drift along naturally with the current, just like the real flies the trout has eaten all its life. You also have a taut, direct connection from rod to fly. It's pretty obvious when a fish takes the fly, and your reaction, setting the hook, is almost instantaneous.

There is an infinite variety of fishing situations, and lots of overlap where fly rods and tenkara rods both work. But when there are intervening currents of varying speeds between you and your fish, using a tenkara rod to reach completely over them can be a very significant advantage.

HOW DO YOU REEL IN A FISH WITH NO REEL?

You point the rod back behind you and pull the fish in close enough to bend down and pick it up or scoop it up in a net. It's that simple.

Sometimes, you need to reach out with your non-rod hand and pull the line to you. I used to think taking the line in hand was disastrous—it disengaged the flex of the rod from the line and made it easy for the fish to break off. But once I started doing it, I learned it works quite well. Usually, it's easy to pull the fish the final few feet to where you can reach it. If the fish decides to mount a last-minute struggle, you can release the line until it settles down, then try again.

CAN YOU CATCH BIG FISH WITH TENKARA?

Yes you can.

Having a reel, with plenty of line in reserve, does afford Western fly fishers a sense of control, of having an action plan when a big fish has taken the fly and is trying to swim away. You can just let the fish pull off the reel as it runs.

With a tenkara rod, the fish can't run. But the rod is flexible enough to bend deeply and absorb the struggles of good-sized trout or bass. Most of the time, this is just as effective as letting a fish pull line from the reel. In fact, too many Western-style fly fishers over-exhaust small trout

The flexibility of a tenkara rod allows it to land good-sized fish efficiently. MORGAN LYLE

by letting them run and pull line when it's really not necessary.

It's true that tenkara is generally a tool for catching average-size trout, say those in the 8- to 14-inch range. When I do manage to hook a larger trout (or a smallmouth bass, which fight much harder), I can usually land it. In the cases I can remember where a good fish has broken me off, it was usually because I didn't have my rod upright enough to provide the big flex.

There are fixed-line rods designed for large fish. In Asia, "pole fishing" is widely used for species ranging from herring to salmon. The rods are as heavy or long as necessary for the size of the fish, but the basic arrangement is the same.

DO YOU NEED TO USE SPECIAL TENKARA FLIES?

No. Most Western- (that is, American and European) style fishing flies work just fine on tenkara rods. The Japanese-style flies that have come to be known as tenkara flies aren't really very different than Western flies, though there are some very cool variations that we'll get into in the chapter on flies.

HOW MUCH DOES IT COST?

One of the nicest things about tenkara fishing is how relatively inexpensive it is. A top-quality fly rod can cost close to $1,000; those labeled "affordable" run $200 to $600. These rods are useless without reels, and a good reel will also cost anywhere from $200 to $500. A fly line alone costs at least $60.

Compared to those prices, tenkara is dirt cheap. The best rods cost under $300, with a few exotic exceptions, and you can get a good rod that will fish well for years for less than $150. A line will set you back only $20 or so, and you don't need to buy a reel at all.

The more expensive rods do cast a little more sweetly than the workaday rods. If you fall in love with tenkara, you may want one. You may also want a small assortment of rods: a shorter, lighter, more nimble one for fishing for brook trout in small mountain streams; a longer, stouter model for fishing weighted flies in larger rivers or lakes; and a 12-foot all-around model for general use. There are different kinds of lines to experiment with, and various kinds of spools to hold them when not in use.

So by the time you've acquired a quiver full of rods and the small items of gear associated with them, you may have invested as much as a decent fly rod and reel or a set of golf clubs. But to start, you can become a tenkara angler for the price of dinner for four at a nice restaurant.

CHAPTER 2

The Story of Tenkara USA

U ntil quite recently, the idea of fly fishing with a rod designed to make short casts, not long ones, was unheard of in the United States and most of Europe. Having lots of line and casting as far as you can was a bedrock principle of sport fishing. If you had asked most American fishermen to give up their ability to make long casts, they would have looked at you like you were crazy.

In April 2009, a twenty-six-year-old banker at Wells Fargo in San Francisco did exactly that, and tenkara arrived in the English-speaking world.

Actually, by April, Daniel Galhardo was already a former banker, having given up a good corporate gig and used his savings to order tenkara rods from three factories in China. He packed them into the tiny Outer Richmond District apartment he shared with his wife, Margaret, launched the Tenkara USA website, and hoped the rods would sell. He figured if he sold one rod every day, he could afford food and rent until tenkara caught on.

Many people did look at Galhardo like he was crazy, but others thought tenkara seemed cool and fun, and the rods did begin to sell. Today, Tenkara USA has sold thousands of rods and is firmly established. So are a half-dozen other tenkara tackle companies.

Americans are using tenkara rods in all fifty states to catch all kinds of fish (to the dismay of purists, who think they should only be used to catch trout, like in Japan). Five years after Tenkara USA launched, the United States, not Japan, was the world's biggest market for tenkara gear.

Daniel Galhardo, founder of Tenkara USA, at the company's office in Boulder, Colorado.
MORGAN LYLE

13

Daniel at Tenkara USA headquarters with an Iwana, the brand's flagship rod. MORGAN LYLE

Using fly rods without reels was the most radical equipment innovation since anglers started using fly rods *with* reels, about three hundred years ago.

Daniel Galhardo grew up in Curitiba, a cosmopolitan state capital with a population of 1.9 million in central Brazil. His parents owned a women's clothing boutique, and entrepreneurship was valued in the family. So was fishing. Weekend outings were spent fishing with simple poles and bait for the local tilapia.

"I remember the rod sticking out the back of the car," Daniel recalled. "I grew up watching all kinds of fishing shows with my dad. On Sunday at 6 a.m., the fishing show would come on and

I would wake him to watch. My dad was always a bait fisherman, still is."

An interesting coincidence is that Curitiba has the second-largest population of people of Japanese origin in the country (only Sao Paolo has more). The local Japanese Brazilians had a reputation as good anglers, and used "either actual cane poles or what we in the States would call a crappie pole," Daniel said.

Daniel soon outgrew simple cane pole fishing. He was attracted to using spinning rods, the most popular rod-and-reel setup today, and to casting artificial lures, not bait, a much craftier way to fish.

As a young teenager, Daniel got wind of fly fishing, which is even craftier. The Internet was rudimentary in the late 1990s and there wasn't much in print about fly fishing in Brazil.

"It took me a ton of research to find a place to buy a fly rod," Daniel said. But eventually he did, and set about figuring out how to cast it. He lucked out and came across some copies of *Fly Fisherman* magazine, which advanced his education in both English and fly fishing.

Daniel spent his senior year of high school as an exchange student in the Central Valley of California. Returning from visiting his folks back in Curitiba, he brought his fly rod to the United States and made some outings to the Sierras, catching his first trout in 2001.

He's been in the States ever since. Daniel enrolled at Santa Barbara City College, transferring to and graduating from the University of San Francisco, with a degree in international business and finance and a minor in Asian studies. He went straight to work at Travelex, a currency-exchange company for travelers. Gainfully employed, he made a beeline for the best-known fly-fishing tackle brand in the US.

"My first paycheck from them, I bought a fly rod from Orvis," he said. "My office was really close to the Orvis shop in downtown San Francisco."

A Revelation in Japan

Daniel moved on to Wells Fargo, and married Margaret in 2007. The following year, the two of them traveled to Japan to visit family and explore the mountains. The trip would involve some backpacking and fishing. It was while researching Japanese fly fishing that Daniel learned of the existence of tenkara. At a tackle shop in Yamagata, he saw a tenkara rod in person for the first time, and was struck by how it

"reminded me of the rods of my childhood, the crappie poles, even though it felt very different."

"My first thought was, 'Wow, that's gonna be great for backpacking,'" he said. The first tenkara rod Galhardo owned was a 3.6-meter (12-foot) Nissin with a cork handle. It came with a line and a spool to stow the line on. Daniel didn't buy any flies because they were expensive, and besides, he already knew how to make his own flies.

At the end of the trip, backpacking buddies picked the couple up at the airport, and Daniel excitedly showed them his Nissin tenkara rod. They weren't diehard anglers like he was, but they were curious. It began to dawn on Daniel that other Americans might be curious, and that he enjoyed explaining tenkara fishing. He thinks of that trip home from the airport as the moment he began thinking of introducing tenkara to the USA.

Not long after, Margaret and Daniel took the tenkara rod to the Sierras. He had purchased it late in his trip to Japan and didn't fish it there; the first place he used it was Mount Lassen National Park in Northern California. Meanwhile, the thought of selling tenkara rods in the United States "kind of brewed for a couple of weeks," he said.

It wasn't the first time a business idea had brewed in Daniel's mind. "I think I just had this desire to start my own thing," he said. "I grew up in a family full of entrepreneurs, and I liked the idea of creating something."

The idea became a project. "I worked my butt off trying to figure out how to make rods," he said, meaning how to contract with factories in Asia to make tenkara rods to his specifications and order them for retail sale in the US. His education and experience in international

Daniel plays a brook trout on Boulder Creek, minutes from his office. The proximity to great trout fishing was one of the factors in the company's move to Boulder from San Francisco. MORGAN LYLE

finance only went so far, and he had to figure out the fishing tackle business as he went. Still, it happened fast. "I think it only took me about seven months to get off the ground and have this stuff figured out. A month before the website was slated to go live, I decided to quit my job and go full time into my business."

TenkaraUSA.com went live in April 2009, establishing the business model every tenkara tackle company would use in the decade to come. In a couple of years, the company's gear would be available in a few brick-and-mortar fly-fishing stores around the country, but the early tenkara was a direct-to-customer online enterprise.

The website was calm and airy, with spare text and lots of white space. Its sales pitch was that fly fishing can be simple and inexpensive. You only need a rod, a line, and a fly, and it's easy and enjoyable to do.

This idea would annoy, if not enrage, some anglers who had been obsessed their whole lives with mastering the intricacies of fly fishing and investing hard-earned money in its gear. But it also embraced the essence of fly fishing, carefully dropping an artificial fly in front of a wary trout in a bucolic mountain stream. It had a clean, modern feel that appealed to young outdoor enthusiasts.

There had been some anticipation in online fishing forums, and Tenkara USA sold a few rods on its first day. It sold about a rod a day during the first week. But then sales went cold, and Daniel got a little panicky. He reached out for publicity from the hook-and-bullet press, and got what turned out to be an important mention by Kirk Deeter and Tim Romano at *Field & Stream*.

The story was picked up by writers who cater to the fly-fishing crowd, including me, and sales resumed. Daniel had a stack of tenkara rods in his apartment for the first six months of the business. At one point, he took a road trip to scout locations for Tenkara USA's first promotional video, and brought rods with him, stopping at local post offices to fulfill them as they came in. (He eventually employed a warehouse-and-order-fulfillment service, restoring order to his and Margaret's living room.)

A month after the launch of Tenkara USA, across the continent in upstate New York, Japanese university professor and prominent tenkara authority Hisao Ishigaki traveled to the Catskill Fly Fishing Center and Museum to give a talk on tenkara fishing. Daniel made sure to attend, and brought a film crew to document the event.

The Catskill Center is a shrine to fly fishing as practiced in the US and Europe. Generations of fly-fishing enthusiasts have had their own culture of celebrities, and many of these fished the Catskills. The publishing houses of Manhattan told their stories in books and magazines, and the Catskills region came to be known, in the words of author Austin McK. Francis, as the birthplace of American fly fishing (to the consternation of other states, which had fly-fishing pioneers of their own).

Daniel and Japanese tenkara expert Hisao Ishigaki at the Catskill Fly Fishing Center and Museum in New York in 2009. DANIEL GALHARDO

Ishigaki gave a talk, translated by Misako Ishimura, who organized the Made in Japan exhibit at the Catskill Center. A small audience of Catskill Center regulars listened politely as Ishigaki explained a way of fly fishing quite different than the one to which they had largely devoted their lives. He also demonstrated how he "tied," or made, the kind of fly he fished with in Japan. Sitting near the preserved fly-tying benches of famous Catskill fly tiers Harry and Elsie Darbee, Walt and Winnie Dette, Lee and Joan Salvato Wulff, Dr. Ishigaki made a fly that was primitive in comparison to the rather complex Catskills patterns. He merely tied a brown rooster feather to a fishhook, wound it around a few times to make its barbs splay out, then wrapped some thread onto the rest of the hook to serve as the elongated body of the insect—a lack of detail that was unthinkable in the twentieth-century heyday of Catskills fly fishing.

It was little more than a mildly interesting afternoon for the Catskills fly-fishing world, but it was important for Daniel. Meeting Ishigaki gave him a connection to the tenkara masters of Japan, which would inform his own knowledge of tenkara and his company's mission of sharing the tackle, technique, and philosophy with customers in the Western world.

Daniel, and other American tenkara influencers, have since made numerous pilgrimages to Japan, fishing and camping with the local tenkara anglers, learning the subtleties of the casting and catching, and becoming familiar with the gear. Ishigaki became a mentor to Daniel, and began making more visits to the US to appear at tenkara gatherings organized by Tenkara USA.

Tenkara USA has its own tenkara mobile, a 2011 Volkswagen van. Here, Daniel rigs up for a little fishing on a local stream with nothing more than a rod and a tiny pack of tackle. MORGAN LYLE

The Casting Contest

It's more than a little ironic that the man who introduced close-range fixed-line fishing to the US once won a distance fly-casting contest.

Daniel won the contest using a two-handed fly rod, a specialty style designed to make especially long casts for large fish like salmon on large rivers. It's pretty much the opposite of tenkara. The contest was held at, and organized by, the Golden Gate Angling and Casting Club, perhaps the world capital of making a really long cast for its own sake. The club's members convinced the Works Progress Administration to build a 400-by-180-foot casting pond in Golden Gate Park in 1938, and phenomenal feats of fly casting have taken place there ever since.

Daniel, in fact, was a member of the board of directors of the club. Living a few blocks away, he would sometimes wander to the casting pond to fly-cast. He began to know a few of the club members on Thanksgiving 2007. A fishing trip with Margaret was scotched by car trouble and the couple ended up hanging around the clubhouse, where they were invited in to dine with club members. Daniel began helping out with the club's monthly casting clinics, and was eventually offered a seat on the board.

"I did win a long-distance casting competition," he said, though claimed not to remember how far he had cast. "I have a medal somewhere. I was not that interested in distance casting. Ever since I came to the States I really was a trout angler, so I wasn't interested in casting far."

He may not have learned how to make "hero casts" at the club, but gained some insight into the way fly fishing looks to people who've never tried it, and it confirmed his worst suspicions. The casting clinics would draw around a hundred people, but most of them never returned.

"A lot of people were really interested in fly fishing and fly casting, because it's a beautiful sport. But a lot of those people wouldn't come back because there was too much going on. 'There's a lot of Latin names and lot of physics, and I go into the fly shop and they're trying to sell me a thousand dollars' worth of gear.'"

His two years on the board, 2008 and 2009, were pleasant enough, but the distance casters didn't quite understand where Daniel was headed with his no-reel rods.

"I always got a little bit of a stinky eye from the people in the club," he said. "I don't think there's a ton of animosity, but I get the sense that they look at me like I'm doing something that shouldn't be done in fly fishing."

Catching On

Tenkara began to pick up steam in the chatty fly-fishing world. Five months after Daniel launched his business, the founder of Patagonia, Yvon Chouinard, published an article extolling tenkara in *Fly Rod & Reel* magazine. It was the first time a big name in the sporting world endorsed tenkara in a major publication. The following summer, Daniel went tenkara fishing with John Gierach, the widely read and universally admired fly-fishing essayist, and magazine writer and author Ed Engle. Neither gave up his fly rod and converted to tenkara, but their willingness to try it lent considerable credibility. Gierach went on to write about tenkara in his column in *Fly Rod & Reel* and adapted the piece to become a chapter in his book *All Fishermen Are Liars*. The *New York Times* published a feature story on tenkara in September 2010.

In 2011, Daniel spent two months learning tenkara in Japan. In September, he organized a tenkara summit in West Yellowstone, Montana, drawing about a hundred people. A few months later, Tenkara USA set up a booth at The Fly Fishing Show, a big expo in Somerset, New Jersey. While there, the most famous fly fisher of the era, the late Bernard "Lefty" Kreh, told Daniel he suspected tenkara was a fad that would fizzle out before long. (Lefty later took it back and said tenkara is a smart way to fish for trout under the right conditions.)

As he was getting ready for that two-month pilgrimage to Japan, Daniel doubled the Tenkara USA workforce by hiring T. J. Ferreira , one of the earliest disciples. Until then, Daniel had been a company of one. As of this writing, T. J. is director of customer service for the company, which is now a team of six full-time employees.

Daniel, Margaret, and Tenkara USA relocated to Boulder, Colorado, in late 2012 to be nearer to trout fishing and to the outdoor-recreation-equipment industry. His first tenkara summit in West Yellowstone was a success, so he held another in Harrisonburg, Virginia, in 2013, and the third in Salt Lake City, Utah, in 2014. Each of these drew over a hundred people.

The 2017 event near Rocky Mountain National Park in Colorado drew over three hundred, Daniel said, from the region and around the country. On Saturday they sat for talks and slide shows, on topics like "Fishing Small Waters" and "Advanced Tenkara," by Ishigaki, Chouinard, and other tenkara luminaries in the Estes Park

Dr. Ishigaki explaining tenkara at the first Tenkara USA summit, alongside the Madison River in Yellowstone National Park. MORGAN LYLE

Daniel demonstrating tenkara at The Fly Fishing Show in Somerset, New Jersey, in January 2012. MORGAN LYLE

Events Center, and fished the RMNP's exquisite trout streams on Sunday.

Tenkara USA's marketing approach was working well. Daniel wasn't out chasing sales; the buzz spread organically in the online forums, kicked along every so often by a new Tenkara USA promotional video or product launch or an article in the fly-fishing press. But the upstart company got a whopping endorsement from the most established company in the fly-fishing industry in July of 2012. The Orvis Co., the company Daniel bought a fly rod from with the first paycheck from his first job after college, added a Tenkara USA rod to its beloved and widely read catalog.

Suddenly a lot of fly fishers who would think it crazy to fish without a reel were seeing tenkara held up as a legitimate way to fish by a company that built its brand on rods and reels.

CHAPTER 3

Fishing in Streams

Trout fishing most often takes place on streams. Tenkara and fly fishing both evolved as methods of catching trout in moving water.

Assuming a given stream provides the proper habitat—unpolluted water that stays below 70 degrees, with a good forage base of aquatic insects—trout will probably live there.

Streams are smart places to fish because they tell us where to cast our flies, by their shape and structure. A large rock with an eddy behind it, the spot where a fast current empties into a slower pool, a run of deeper water along a bank under a shade tree: These are obvious places to try. A pond keeps its secrets, but a stream gives you clues.

We also fish streams because they are beautiful places to be. Moving water, and especially water rushing around stones, is endlessly fascinating. It is both calming and quietly exciting. Walled in by trees or carved into a meadow, the water steps down to the sea one tiny waterfall at a time, sunshine glinting and shimmering on the surface, currents braiding and pooling, each tiny interruption of the flow a potential hiding spot for a trout. Throw in the actual signs of life, the splashes and dimples of feeding trout, and you are presented with what seems like infinite possibility, a never-ending series of exquisite challenges.

Fly fishers like to say the "tug is the drug," meaning the pull of a hooked fish, but I'm equally addicted to the water itself. As the writer Roderick Haig-Brown once wrote, "Perhaps fishing is, for me, only an excuse to be near rivers. If so, I'm glad I thought of it."

The South Platte River in Colorado is a picture-perfect trout stream: clean and cold, with lots of places to hide and lots of aquatic organisms to eat. MORGAN LYLE

Walking in the Water

We're talking here about brooks, creeks, small rivers—streams that would be among the first five or six orders in the Strahler scientific classification scale. In other words: wadeable streams—streams small enough for a person to walk in. They have deep spots as well as shallow spots, but you can generally get around on foot.

The Environmental Protection Agency says there are more than 670,000 miles of wadeable streams in the US. That's 90 percent of the rivers and streams in the country. They are the capillaries of the nation's aquatic vascular system, a coast-to-coast lacework that services the big veins and arteries like the Hudson, the Mississippi, and the Colorado. Living in such streams are insects that live nowhere else, uniquely adapted to the environment, subsisting on vegetation that falls from nearby trees and grasses or grows on the streambed stones. With any luck, as far as the angler is concerned, the food chain extends upward to include fish, particularly trout, that feed on the flies.

Not every wadeable stream has fish in it. The proper habitat is required. For trout, that means clean water that seldom is warmer than 70 degrees, and the colder, the better. For a trout population to be self-sustaining—that is, not stocked by government agencies or private

Adam Klagsbrun tightens up on a brown trout that took his *kebari*, or trout fly, on Boulder Creek in Colorado. MORGAN LYLE

One advantage of tenkara fishing is that you can hold the light line above the water with the long rod, so the line doesn't get swept downstream by the current and pull your fly off course. SUSAN EPSTEIN

landowners—habitat suitable for spawning is also required, such as beds of clean gravel in which trout can make nests for their eggs.

These conditions are most often found in the higher elevations. Streams formed in ravines, from rain and melting snow flowing downhill as well as groundwater welling up from seeps and springs, are perfect for trout, and trout are perfect for them. The most trout streams are found in the Appalachian, Rocky, and Sierra mountain regions.

If you live in the northern half of the country or even the southern half on either side, you're probably no more than a couple hours' drive from good trout fishing.

Many of these streams are inside state and national parks and are generally open to fishing. We Americans are incredibly fortunate to have so many miles of streams available for our recreation. Many more miles of streams aren't in parks but are accessible, thanks to the willingness of landowners or because government conservation agencies have purchased easements from the property owners for the purpose of allowing anglers on their land.

Tenkara is trout fishing, by definition; it describes the practice of fishing for trout in streams with a fixed-line rod. You could use a fixed-line rod for other kinds of fishing, but it wouldn't be tenkara any more than kicking a

Tenkara also works well on streams that are too deep to wade, or on ponds or lakes if you have a boat.

GEORGE AND AMIDEA DANIEL

basketball around on a soccer pitch would be playing basketball. As it happens, many American anglers enjoy using fixed-line rods, but don't live conveniently close to trout waters. They have wadeable streams nearby, but the fish in them tend to be species that thrive in warmer waters, like bass, crappie, bluegill, pickerel, sunfish, pike, and carp. You can use your tenkara rod to fish for these species. It's not tenkara, strictly speaking, but it's a fun and effective way to fish.

When and Where to Fish

Trout live in cool, clean waters. Some regions have a great many of them, like the Mountain West, the Pacific Northwest, the upper Midwest, and the northeastern and mid-Atlantic states. Trout fishing is also found farther south, in the southern Appalachians and the Ozarks, or in those areas of the Southwest that have cool water, such as higher elevations or rivers downstream of dams, where cold water is released from deep reservoirs.

Few outdoor sports capture the imagination of participants as thoroughly as trout fishing. The appeal is multifaceted; we love the beautiful fish and the beautiful places they live, and we love the game of trying to overcome their wary survival instincts by enticing them to bite an artificial fly. Wading the stream, studying the water, knowing how trout feed, and using a long, willowy rod and light line to present a fly in just the right way: It's interesting, it's exciting, it's utterly absorbing. You live in hope it will work. You still enjoy the game greatly even when it doesn't.

The basic structure of the game is that trout spend most of their time facing upstream, waiting to pick off aquatic insects that come drifting down to them. Your challenge is to make a trout think your fly is one of those insects—or at least that your fly is close enough to a real insect to be worth a try. The only way to try is for the fish to grab the potential snack in its mouth—and then you've caught it.

Tenkara is ideal for this kind of fishing. Especially in swiftly flowing water, with lots of rocks and eddies, you can sneak up pretty close to a feeding trout, either from the shore or by wading in the stream, so the fact that your casting distance is limited doesn't matter. You don't need a reel full of line to reach a trout twenty feet away—and it's not hard to get within twenty feet of a trout in a rushing stream. You simply flick a fly into or onto the water ahead of where you think the trout may be, let it drift downstream and be ready for the bite.

The Trout Angler's Seasons

Trout-fishing success is often a matter of being in the right place at the right time. The right place is easy enough to figure out; some very casual research will reveal the good trout

Adam Reiger ties on a fly while fishing the Farmington River in Connecticut. Fed by water from the base of a tall dam, the Farmington stays cold and trout friendly all summer. SUSAN EPSTEIN

streams in your locality. The right time is fairly straightforward, too: from early to mid-spring, depending where you live, through fall. Early morning and evening are the best times of day. Fishing can be slow in the heat of summer, unless you have access to streams that stay cold all year. Trout fishing is possible in the winter, but the action is much slower.

Good trout fishing starts when water temperatures rise above 50 degrees. In southern areas, this happens as early as March, while the most northern regions may not see 50-degree water until sometime in May. Trout eat heartily at this time of year because their metabolisms have awakened from the lethargy of winter, and because the insects on which they feed also become active once the stream temps are in the 50s.

So once the temperature of your local trout stream is anywhere between the low 50s and the mid 60s, the fishing should be good.

In the natural course of things, the water will continue to warm as weeks go by, and in many places stream temperatures will approach or even exceed 70 degrees by midsummer. That's usually the cutoff point. Trout become lethargic again in warm water, and catch-and-release fishing is not a good idea in such conditions; the ordeal of being caught could be fatal, even if the fish initially swims away seemingly unharmed when you let it go. At that point, if you want to fish, it's better to pursue fish that thrive in warmer water, like bass or panfish (crappie, perch, sunfish, bluegill, pickerel, etc.).

In the fall, as streams begin to cool off, good fishing returns, and will persist until water temperatures begin to sink through the low 40s and into the 30s.

Forever Spring, below the Dams

If you have access to a river downstream of a dam, you might have cold water all summer. Known as tailwaters or tailraces, this kind of stream stays cold because water is released from the base of the dam, where the water is coldest. The tailwater I'm most familiar with is the upper Delaware River, where water coming out of the dams on its two branches can be a bit below 50 degrees all summer. It's forever spring on the Delaware; the conditions are so good that the state doesn't even bother stocking it with trout raised in hatcheries. The wild trout thrive to the point where they reproduce well enough on their own that human intervention isn't necessary.

In the Mountain West, there's an interesting wrinkle to the fishing schedule. Streams begin to warm in April as they do in other places, and fishing gets underway in similar fashion. But as summer sets on, the snow pack in the peaks begins to melt, and the rush of the melting snow turns the rivers into deep, cold torrents. Fish survive this phenomenon just fine, but fishing becomes difficult if not impossible, and Rocky Mountain anglers usually need to wait again for the streams to settle down before resuming their fishing.

Spring is when the aquatic insects "hatch" en masse. That's the fly-fishing term for the metamorphosis of the mayflies, caddisflies, and stoneflies that were born the year before. In spring, they ascend to the surface, change to winged insects, and leave the stream, only to return in a day or three for the mating swarm and egg-laying that produces the next year's crop.

Fish feed eagerly when this goes on. The hatches continue throughout the fishing season, with regional variations, but the activity is so concentrated in the spring that the late fishing writer Art Lee once described it as a baseball season that begins with the World Series. If you can fish when water temperatures are in the upper 50s and the hatches are in full swing, you'll experience some of the best fishing of the year.

But even in the prime time for hatches, the actual event is usually limited to an hour or two, sometimes in the afternoon, sometimes in the evening. And on many days, a full-on hatch doesn't happen at all. This doesn't mean you can't have good fishing—it just means you have to go find the fish and figure out a way to entice them. Tenkara fishing is excellent for this situation. Japanese tenkara anglers are famously uninterested in matching the hatch and being on the water at the exact time of peak hatching activity. They don't worry about having a fly that closely imitates the real bugs. They concentrate on stealthily putting a fly where a fish will see it and making sure it does what they want it to, whether that means letting it drift naturally with the current or giving it life by making it move in the water.

CHAPTER 4

Ed Van Put and the Japanese Rod

In 1998, the man who would one day introduce tenkara fishing to the Western world was still a teenager in Brazil. But a decade before the launch of Tenkara USA, a few American fly-fishing luminaries had gotten wind of tenkara and were quietly experimenting on their local streams.

One of them was Dave Hughes, the author of many wonderful fly-fishing books, an authority whose expertise is unquestioned (and who greatly influenced my own development as a fly fisher). Hughes's wife, Masako, is Japanese, and he learned about tenkara while visiting Japan in the early 1980s.

Another was Yvon Chouinard, founder of the worldwide Patagonia outdoor gear brand and longtime surfer, climber, and fly fisher, who had also fished with a tenkara rod for years before they became widely known in the West. Chouinard coauthored a 2014 book, *Simple Fly Fishing: Techniques for Tenkara and Rod & Reel*, and began selling a tenkara rod at Patagonia's stores and website.

And there was Ed Van Put.

Having grown up fly fishing in the Catskill Mountains, Ed was something of a hero to me. First I read about him in Austin McK. Francis's book, *Land of Little Rivers*. Then I read Ed's own books, *The Beaverkill* and *Trout Fishing in the Catskills*. As a journalist covering fly fishing who often interviewed Ed for his expertise, I eventually got to know him personally.

Van Put's books are magnificent, but he wrote them on the side. His day job was fisheries professional for the New York State Department of Environmental Conservation. In that role he advocated for rules that required New York City to release

---

Renowned Catskill Mountains author, angler, and conservationist Ed Van Put began experimenting (successfully) with tenkara in 1998. MORGAN LYLE

Ed spent his career with the New York Department of Environmental Conservation, but he may be best known for his superb histories, including *The Beaverkill: The History of a River and Its People*. MORGAN LYLE

cold water from reservoirs on dammed Catskills rivers, which created some of the best trout fisheries in the country, downstream of the dams.

Equally if not more important, Ed convinced many landowners in the Catskills to sell easements to New York State, so that anglers could legally access the trout streams on their lands. Many miles of exquisite fishing are available to anyone with a fishing license, thanks to his efforts.

In the course of his career, Van Put came to know as much as anyone, and more than most, about trout and trout fishing, particularly in his home region. He and his wife, Judy Van Put, a real estate agent who is also an accomplished angler, give talks and slide shows to fishing clubs. When former president Jimmy Carter came to the Catskills to do some fishing, it was Ed who guided him, sharing his knowledge of the local streams.

Ed was a member of the inner circle of Catskills guides, outfitters, tackle-shop owners, writers, and fly tiers. This group founded the Catskill Fly Fishing Center and Museum, a world-class facility along the Willowemoc River. Ed was soon inducted into the center's Hall of Fame, among a roster of the most famous fly fishers, past and present, from around the world.

Ed's mother, Agnes Van Put, age 102 at this writing, works part-time at the center, which is just down the road from Ed's house. (Ed's not in the Hall of Fame because his mom is on the payroll, and Agnes doesn't work there because her son is in the Hall. They both earned their positions.) Agnes has made soup and cookies for the public on the opening day of trout season for many years.

I first heard of tenkara in April of 2009, when Tenkara USA opened for business. A month later, by pure coincidence, the Catskill Center hosted an exhibit and presentation on fly fishing in Japan. The guest speaker was Dr. Hisao Ishigaki, one of the most prominent Japanese tenkara anglers, who had written articles and produced videos on the sport. This was almost certainly the first public event dedicated to tenkara in the United States, and perhaps anywhere outside of Japan.

I covered the presentation. Agnes was there. We were chatting.

"Ed's had one of those Japanese rods for years," she said.

Tenkara before Tenkara Was Cool

It turns out Ed had gotten his hands on what is technically known as a *keiryu* rod and gone on something of a rampage on the local streams eleven years earlier, during which he introduced tenkara to a whole bunch of American trout.

Jimmy Carter wasn't the only prominent person to have hired Ed Van Put as a guide. Paul Volcker, chairman of the Federal Reserve during the presidencies of Carter and Ronald Reagan, also engaged Van Put's services. Tagging along with Volcker was Seiichiro Otsuka, the Japanese ambassador to the United States.

Correspondence between Ed and Ambassador Seiichiro Otsuka. MORGAN LYLE

Ed looks over the fiberglass rod given to him by a former Japanese ambassador to the United States. The rod is technically a *keiryu* or "mountain stream" rod, designed to be fished with bait, but Ed used a fly instead. MORGAN LYLE

They had such a good time that the ambassador subsequently hired Ed again, in June 1998, to take him, his wife, and his son fishing.

"He spoke flawless English, he went to school in America, had stayed with people in Minnesota, and was the ambassador to this country and his office was in Manhattan," Van Put recalled. "He fished traditional Western tackle, and was as good as any fly fisherman I knew with Western tackle."

The fishing party proceeded to Beaverkill Falls, a picturesque pool on a privately owned stretch of the river to which Van Put had access due to his longstanding connections.

At one point, the ambassador "said he wanted to go get a Japanese rod," Van Put said. "And he came down with two or three rods, made out of telescoping graphite and fiberglass, and from 12 to 18 feet, and he was catching one fish after another. And the large graphite rod—he said, 'Here, you try it,' and I just dropped the fly in the water and moved it a little bit and I caught a rainbow trout."

His first time fishing a fixed-line rod was revelatory for Van Put. At the end of the trip, Ambassador Otsuka gave Ed a rod, a *keiryu* rod made of fiberglass. He did not become a convert; he continued to do most of his fishing with

Pine Creek in the Catskills, one of the smaller streams Van Put fished with his Japanese rod. MORGAN LYLE

a fly rod. But the novelty and the effectiveness of the Japanese "mountain stream rod," as the ambassador called it, captured his fancy for the early summer of 1998.

Ed was taken by the intimacy of the gear. Even more than in regular fly fishing, the rod and line felt like an extension of his arm and hand. Its primitive design reminded Ed of the way famed nineteenth-century naturalist John Burroughs fished as a boy: "They would cut a willow, tie a piece of line onto it, and that's how they fished. At the end of the day you threw it away."

No doubt many of the Japanese *shokuryoshi*, or commercial stream fishermen, fished the same way, halfway around the world, during the same era. Burroughs's rod was willow, while the Japanese version was bamboo, but either way, it was all that was needed to catch trout in mountain streams.

When I fished with Ed in 2013, he used a custom-made fiberglass 4-weight fly rod, rigged with an old-fashioned double-taper fly line, rather than the more aggressive forward-taper lines used by most fly fishers today. That's still how he fishes most of the time. But during the weeks after being given a rod by the Japanese ambassador, Ed's fly rod collected dust; he went on a fixed-line fishing binge on some of the very streams Burroughs fished as a boy growing up in Roxbury, New York.

"It was kind of nice, because I likened what I was doing to the way Burroughs fished," he said.

Van Put stalked Burroughs's waters in the northwestern Catskills, and the streams closer to home that he knew from his own decades of fishing and stewardship. The Pine Kill. The Mongaup. The Beaverkill. Trout Brook. Russell Brook. Abe Wood Brook. Stewart Brook. He caught fish on all of them, and he wrote down what happened.

Using the Japanese stream-trout rod the ambassador had given him, Ed caught twenty wild brown trout and one wild brookie on June 25, using a size 12 Royal Coachman wet fly, in three hours. Ed kept detailed notes of his fishing—species, origin, size, fly, location, conditions.

"Fished Mongaup Creek (above hatchery)," reads one notebook entry. "Caught 5 wild S.T. [state biologist lingo for brook trout]. 1 wild B.T. [brown trout]. Largest S.T. 10¼, B.T. 11½, #12 Royal Coachman. [Below hatchery] 5 wild S.T. 1 hatchery B.T. approx. 13" #12 Royal Coachman. Used Japanese Mt. Stream rod."

It goes on for page after page. One page of the datebook where he kept his notes had no entry. "May have gone to work that day," Ed said with a laugh.

Technically, what Ed was doing wasn't quite tenkara fishing. A *keiryu* rod works the same way as a tenkara rod—telescoping, with the line tied directly to the tip—but is designed for bait fishing with an insect larva or a worm and a split BB or two to help it sink. A tenkara angler casts an unweighted fly, much the way a fly fisher does. Ed used a split shot for a sinker, but his bait was the Royal Coachman fly.

His approach, however, was pure tenkara. He made no attempt to trick his trout with a fly designed to imitate any particular species of insect. He relied instead on technique, using the long rod and light line to stealthily drop a fly where his know-how told him trout were likely to be holding, waiting for something to eat to come drifting by.

There was a lot of rain in June 1998, and the streams were rather swollen all month. Ed stalked the pools, approaching carefully, dropping his fly into promising water.

"That's when it's a killer—when that stream is up and dirty, it's dynamite," Ed said. "This particular summer it stayed up all summer, and that's why I went nuts with this thing.

"Now it's every day I'm going," he said, and began reading from his notes as we sat at the kitchen counter in his house in Livingston Manor, New York. "'Fished Scudder Brook'— which is in Hardenburgh, above Lew Beach— 'fifteen minutes, caught one wild brook trout Royal Coachman 12, one hatchery brook trout, one wild brown . . .

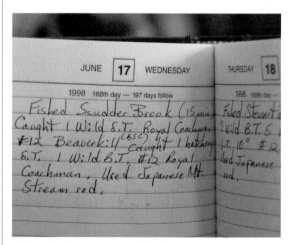

Ed Van Put's notes from his first summer trout fishing with a *keiryu* rod. MORGAN LYLE

"'Stewart Brook, caught seven wild brown trout, five wild brook trout, largest 10 inches, number 12 Royal Coachman, used Japanese mountain rod. Fished Mongaup Creek'—that's below the hatchery in Debruce—'caught five brown trout, two hatchery, three wild, largest 14 inches. Three wild brook trout, largest 10 inches. One rainbow trout, hatchery, 9 inches. Number 12 Royal Coachman. Fished Henry Brook'—that's right by the hatchery—'caught nine wild brook trout, number 12 Royal Coachman, largest 8.' Then I was getting really carried away."

The Japanese rod odyssey culminated in July, with two great days on Trout Brook. Ed then paused to tally his success.

"Here I added up, six days, I caught 76 rainbows, 43 brook trout, and 12 brown trout, a total of 132. So that is like 21 fish a trip. I mean I was going crazy," he said, again laughing.

I pointed out to Ed that he's a very accomplished fly fisher. "Don't you think you would have caught those 132 with a regular rod and reel?" I asked.

"No way," he said. "No way. Because I'm on the bottom. The streams are high. Some are dirty, some aren't dirty, but they're high. And this is sneaky. You know, you walk up, you don't really get in the water unless you absolutely have to, and you sort of swing it ahead of you, it goes to the bottom, it comes along at a nice slow speed, and you're just staying in contact with the split shot, and if it hesitates, you set the hook. With fly line, when that line comes down, there's a disturbance. However insignificant it can be, it's still a disturbance, it's an unnatural thing. But this split shot, you just lower it into the water. Sometimes you don't even cast it. It's sneaky!"

Again, he was laughing, still surprised twenty years later by the effectiveness of this improbable gear. Like most fly fishers (and tenkara fishers), Ed releases the trout he catches, but he wondered aloud what would happen should a less conservation-minded angler get hold of a Japanese rod. "I mean, Morgan, it's like, my God, what if everybody did this! I thought, jokingly, that they shouldn't let people fish with this."

Big Fish on Light Rods

The streams Ed fished that summer were mainly small ones, twenty- or thirty-feet wide, not those big, famous Catskills rivers like the Beaverkill or the Delaware. His trout topped out around a foot in length in keeping with the size of the streams themselves; small streams always hold a few large trout, but most are of modest size.

In this, Ed had much in common with Japanese trout fishers, since trout generally run smaller in Japan than the US, or at least smaller than in large American rivers. That fact does not deter American tenkara fishers from bringing their fixed-line rods where they might catch really big trout, and Ed was no exception.

"I caught a 19-inch trout on Stewart Brook with it. But I was lucky because in a small stream, a big fish stays in the pool. With that fish, there was a meadow in the side I was fishing on, so I was free to walk up and down until I had worn him out.

"But I remember telling [Ambassador Otsuka] that I caught a 16-inch fish, and he said, 'On that rod?' Like I shouldn't be using it.

"You can't determine what's going to take a fly. But I use 4X measured from the tip to the base of the rod, then I fish with 6X," he said. (4X is 4-pound test line, while 6X breaks at 2 pounds of pressure.) "I'm just thinking that if anything's going to break, it's going to be the 6X—not the rod."

Ed still does most of his fishing with a fly rod. He caught this handsome rainbow on a fall day on the East Branch of the Delaware River. MORGAN LYLE

At one point, Ed's Japanese mountain stream rod did break. A local rod maker managed to repair it with segments of fiberglass, but couldn't match the color. You can still see the pale, mismatched bands of fiberglass in the rod today.

"When it broke, and I had no way of repairing it, I mean I was devastated," he said. "This was my initial rod, and I have so many memories of it. When you think about it, it's like, how the heck did they make this? It's incredible that they would even think of doing this.

"And there's no name on it, and I didn't know what to do. I had a friend who was in Japan and he looked around and he couldn't find them. And I wrote to the ambassador, and he

sent me this back," he said, showing me a paper with contact info for Daiwa, the Japanese-based global tackle brand. Daiwa apparently didn't make his rod, but they certainly made plenty of *keiryu* rods.

"I contacted Daiwa. You know what they told me? They don't send them to America. They didn't sell them in the US. I think they just were not popular."

That's true. By 1998, I had been an avid fly fisher for a long time. I read every article in every magazine. I had never heard of a fly rod that didn't use a reel.

Ed contacted Daiwa and was informed that because the company had no established distribution channel to the United States, he'd have to buy six rods to justify the international shipment. So he did. He gave two to fisheries colleagues, two to his sons, and kept the other two. Unlike the original rod given to him by Ambassador Otsuka, the Daiwa rods would look very familiar to many American tenkara anglers today: made of pale gray graphite with no cork handle, and designed to be fished at any of three lengths: 3.6 meters (11.8 feet), 4.0 meters (13.1 feet), or 4.4 meters (14.4 feet).

Dave Hughes, Yvon Chouinard, and Ed Van Put all fell in love with tenkara, but only for specific purposes on specific streams. None of them swore off their fly rods and converted to full-time tenkara fishing. Ed likes the Japanese rod early in the season, when streams run high and trout are down deep, feeding on whatever aquatic insects they have access to. But if mayflies are "hatching" in great numbers on the broad, flat pools of the East Branch of the Delaware, and the river's chunky trout are sipping them from the surface, Ed will fish for them with his fly rod, pulling line from his reel to make graceful 50-foot casts. Some American fly fishers have become tenkara-only purists, but for others, tenkara only goes so far.

When it works, however, it works great.

"I think my most enjoyable part of this rod was learning how many fish are in some of these streams," Ed said. "I had fished them all with a fly rod, but never, ever caught what I caught with this rod. Never. Like I said, to me it was like doing a fishery survey. You say, 'holy Christ, look at all the fish in here.'"

CHAPTER 5

Fishing with Flies

The aquatic insects upon which trout feed spend most of their lives as crawling bugs among the streambed rocks. At some point, they ascend to the surface of the stream, where they metamorphose, sprouting wings and flying off to the streamside brush for the short, final phase of their lives, usually no more than a couple of days. Now terrestrial insects, they mate, fly back to the stream, and lay their fertilized eggs, which sink to the bottom and will become the next generation of mayflies, stoneflies, or caddisflies.

When these insects leave the safety of the streambed rocks and float to the surface—sometimes in great numbers—for the transition to the next phase of their lives, they are vulnerable to trout, who pick them off on or just below the surface. This is why much trout fishing is done within just a few inches of the surface. It's why trout spend so much of their time "looking up."

However, if no "hatch" is taking place and the trout have no reason to be feeding near the surface, the best way to catch them is with flies designed to sink down near the bottom.

A handful of simple flies can be used for each of these situations. They fall into three categories: dry flies, wet flies, and nymphs. Dry flies float. Wet flies drift along underwater, not far below the surface. Nymphs also drift along underwater, but usually near the bottom. In general, all of them are meant to suggest aquatic insects, and they tend to be about ¼- to ½-inch long.

That's a Killer Bug fly in the trout's mouth, and a Tenkara USA Ebisu rod in the background. MORGAN LYLE

Dry-Fly Fishing

Casting floating flies to trout feeding at the surface is nothing less than an obsession for a legion of fly fishers, and has been for generations. It really is thrilling to see a trout come up and snatch your fly from the surface. You need to drop the fly upstream, so that it drifts down right over the fish. And for the most part, the fly needs to look like the real bugs the fish are eating.

Now, "looks like" is a concept that has been called into question from time to time. The tenkara era is one of those times. We tenkara anglers tend to think artificial flies that vaguely suggest the naturals are preferable to the patterns developed over decades to be supposedly precise imitations. But whichever idea you subscribe to, the procedure is the same: Drop your fly lightly on the water and make sure it drifts naturally—what we call a "dead drift."

A fly rod and reel allow you to do this kind of fishing at a considerable distance: 30, 40, 50 feet away, even longer if you're an accomplished caster. But it also presents the biggest

The Deer Hair Sedge, a simple imitation of a caddisfly that works well anytime trout are feeding at the surface. MORGAN LYLE

disadvantage of fly fishing: The fly line is lying on the water. It is subject to the effect of intervening currents between the angler and the fly, creating drag, and it also scares fish.

Tenkara dry-fly fishing must be done at close range, but if you can reach the fish, it works great. If you use a level line, you can hold the whole line and most of the tippet off the surface—virtually nothing on the water but the fly. It's the stealthiest possible presentation. And because you have a "tight" line with no slack, you usually don't have to set the hook. The fish hooks itself upon grabbing the fly.

Furled lines can also be used for dry-fly fishing. They are heavier than level lines and therefore difficult to hold entirely off the water. But they're also really sweet to cast, and most of the time you only have a few feet of the line and the tippet on the water, which is still less obtrusive than a standard fly line. Furled lines can be especially helpful in windy conditions. A fly line lying on the water can actually be helpful if it's really windy, and not just for dry flies but

Mayflies are a big part of a trout's diet on many streams, and many artificial flies are designed to resemble or suggest them. MORGAN LYLE

for flies of all kinds. It "anchors" the tippet and fly, where a line held off the water would blow out of control.

Some people like using floating lines for dry-fly fishing. These are essentially miniature fly lines, usually untapered, sold specifically for use with tenkara rods. They do present the disadvantages of fly lines: They can scare fish, they are subject to being pulled by currents, and they absorb clues that fish have taken the fly. But if what you enjoy is dry-fly fishing on flat pools, you can negate all these disadvantages. Use a long leader and fish close first, so as you cast progressively farther away, the floating line lands on water where you have determined there are no fish (or at least no fish that care about your dry fly). In smooth, flat water,

intervening currents may not be a problem at all. And you don't need clues about when a fish takes your fly. Surface takes are obvious.

Wet-Fly Fishing

If you're interested in authentic Japanese-style fishing, wet flies are what you'll use. The original subsistence tenkara fishers in Japan used wet flies, and so did all original fly fishers worldwide. In its simplest form—and that's the kind those old *shokuryoshi* used—a wet fly has a body made of thread or wool wrapped onto the shank of a hook, and feather fibers protruding from the front of the fly. These two features suggest the insect's elongated body and its appendages (legs, antennae, wings, and so forth).

This Massachusetts brown trout was feeding on caddisflies, and took a Deer Hair Emerger without hesitation. MORGAN LYLE

As simple as it is, this kind of wet fly can do a very good job of suggesting an aquatic insect that has left behind its life as a rock-crawling nymph and is ascending to the surface to become a winged insect. Wet flies usually have no weight other than the steel of the hook itself, so they tend to run shallow; absent any special effort to get it to sink deeper, a wet fly will drift along a few inches below the surface. That's fine. Lots of trout can be found within a few inches of the surface and will gladly grab the *kebari*.

You can use a wet fly any way you can imagine. Cast it into stony "pocketwater" and let it wash around rocks and through eddies. Look for a "run" of deep water with current at a walking pace and a slightly choppy surface and drift your fly through it, casting as far upstream of the run as you can to give the fly maximum time to sink. You can fish your fly deeply in a pool with more patient sink-waiting, letting your whole tippet go below the surface to allow the fly to get near the bottom.

A time-honored fly-fishing strategy uses a wet fly when fish are feeding near, but not quite on, the surface. The situation is that you see the splashes and bulges of feeding trout, but the fish don't seem to be eating floating flies—real ones or yours. Trout sometimes seem to have a decided preference for ascending nymphs that haven't yet reached the surface. The bugs may have already begun struggling out of their nymphal shucks, and would look quite a bit like our *kebari* with its feather fibers wiggling

Fishing simple wet flies like these a few inches below the surface is the essence of tenkara. Their slim bodies and hackle collars suggest the key features of aquatic insects. MORGAN LYLE

Adam Klagsbrun ties on a *kebari* while fishing in Colorado. MORGAN LYLE

around in the water. This is a great situation for a wet fly, drifting helplessly a few inches below the surface.

The most fun way to fish with a wet fly is *kebari* manipulation, which is covered in the chapter on tenkara fishing techniques.

Nymph Fishing

Nymphs differ from dry flies in that they're designed to sink, and from wet flies in that they usually don't have much in the way of appendages. They're mostly just a "body." Some are made of nothing more than yarn wrapped onto a hook. Others are more elaborate, but they all seek to imitate a wingless, crawling bug, usually one with a segmented abdomen. They are meant to imitate mayflies, caddisflies, and stoneflies in the stage of their lives where they live among the rocks of the streambed. Many nymph patterns have lead or lead-substitute wire wrapped on their hooks before the rest of the fly's dressing to give them weight that helps them sink. Many have heads made of metal beads.

In the early years of American fly fishing, wet flies and then dry flies were the most widely used kinds; nymphs were an afterthought or a last resort. That changed in the last few decades of the twentieth century, when nymphing came to be seen as both the most reliable way to catch fish (since it didn't depend on the trout responding to a "hatch" of insects), and a challenging and intriguing game.

It's thought by many that trout are skittish near the surface, where they face more danger from predators like fish hawks and ospreys, and are less cautious in their safe havens down in the depths. If something comes drifting by that could be an insect, they'll grab it. Fly-fishing guides often set up clients who are new to fly fishing with nymphing rigs, because it's the most likely way to get them into some fish. Competition fly fishers fish with nymphs most of the time, simply because that's the surest way to get fish on their scorecard.

Nymphs are not considered traditional tenkara flies, although lots of tenkara anglers in Japan enjoy using them. Because of their weight, they're a little ungainly on most true tenkara rods. Several models of *keiryu* rods, however, are stiff enough to cast the heavier flies with ease and, importantly, to set the hook when a fish down in several feet of water takes a fly. You can use a stiffer rod for your nymph fishing, or you can simply adjust your technique with your regular tenkara rod to compensate for the weight of the fly.

It's extremely tempting to fish nymphs with a tenkara (or *keiryu*) rod. It's probably the kind of fly I have used the most when fixed-line fishing. The line held aloft by the long rod, angling sharply down through the surface, helps nymphs to sink and allows them to drift naturally while staying in close touch. If a fish touches your fly (or for that matter if your fly bangs into a rock or log) you'll see the line halt or twitch immediately, and usually feel it almost as quickly. That allows you to set the hook before the trout figures out the fly is fake and spits it out. The control and sensitivity are great.

At least in theory, you can boost your chances by fishing with two different nymphs. If the trout don't like the one, maybe they'll like the other. Or maybe the first one will serve to get their attention and the second will tempt them to bite. It makes the most sense to use nymphs that differ in color and size. After all, if the trout didn't want the first Killer Bug, why would it be interested in the second? A better choice might be a size 12 Killer Bug with a size 18 Pheasant Tail trailing it.

It's not considered part of authentic Japanese tenkara, but using multiple flies has been common in fly fishing for hundreds of years. In *The Angler and the Loop Rod*, published in 1885, David Webster wrote that he used nine flies at a time. That strikes me as begging for trouble.

Nymphs can be big or small, heavy or light. They're all designed to tempt fish holding near the bottom to bite. MORGAN LYLE

"Swimming" a streamer is a good way to cover water on a large river. Use the rod to twitch the fly through the water, or let the current swing it across. JOE MCDONOUGH

You run an increased risk of tangles just using two flies. Still, many fly fishers and some tenkara anglers swear by it.

There are various ways to rig up two (or even three) nymphs on the same tippet. The simplest, and the one I use most often, is to tie on a nymph, then tie 18 inches of tippet to the bend of the nymph's hook and tie another nymph onto the end of that. Some anglers prefer the old-fashioned method of tying the flies to droppers, or short lengths of tippet tied perpendicular to the main. There are various ways to make those, too; the simplest I know of is to tie on another length of tippet and leave a long excess tag end, to which you tie the fly.

You need to go easy when casting multiple nymphs to avoid tangles. Keep the "loop" in your cast open wider than you would when casting just one fly, and slow the pace of the back and forward casts a bit. Then again, you shouldn't be making tenkara casts with much force anyway. Use a light touch; you have 12 feet (or more) of springy carbon fiber ready to fling your line and fly, or flies, at your command.

Streamer Fishing

I don't love fishing with streamers on tenkara rods. I do it sometimes, and I do catch fish. I also sometimes fish wet flies or nymphs as if they were streamers, and that works, too. But I think of streamers—flies designed to resemble small fish instead of insects—as being best suited to a fly rod, where you can cast them a long way and then pull the line back in to make them swim through a significant length of water.

It's also true that most streamers are, by tenkara standards, heavy. Modern streamer experts are designing and tying flies that are nearly as big as a lot of the trout I catch, and too heavy and bulky to cast with a tenkara rod. Some of them are heavy enough to cast with a spinning rod. Tenkara gear is ideal for drifting "insect" flies, but not for hucking big-bait fish patterns.

Even so, sometimes you just want to fish a Woolly Bugger. For one thing, it's a more effective way to target large fish. Older and bigger trout do eat flies, but they're also more likely than small trout to look for larger meals like minnows, crayfish, and other underwater critters that pack more calories than mayfly or caddisfly nymphs.

Trout are also thought to bite streamers out of anger as well as hunger. A small, fish-like creature straying into a big brown's territory might seem like a provocation. The response is often aggression, which translates to a hard, confident strike.

So it is worthwhile for the tenkara trout fisher to have some streamers on hand. It's even more worthwhile when you're fishing for bass and other warmwater predators. They eat insects, too, but the best way to catch them is with something bigger and more annoying than a *kebari*.

Fishing a streamer on a tenkara rod is very simple: Cast the fly to one edge of the water you want to cover, let it sink as deep as you think it should, then twitch and swim it through the water by pulling the line with the tip of the rod. If you're fishing water that's downstream of you, it's even simpler: Cast across and let the fly swing across the current. This, by the way, is how most fly fishing was done for centuries, with whatever flies were available at the time. Casting upstream is a relatively recent technique.

Of course, you can't swim a streamer very far with a tenkara rod. But if you pick a spot that's likely to be holding a fish, you probably only need to swim the fly a few feet anyway.

Stillwater Fishing

Tenkara evolved as a way to fish moving water, but it can be used to fish stillwaters, too. Whether it's bass and bluegills in a farm pond or trout in a high-elevation alpine lake, you can catch on a fixed-line rod.

The main difference, of course, is that the water in a lake or pond isn't moving. If your fly is going to move, you have to move it yourself. That's not always necessary; if you have rising trout within casting range, for example, you can cast a dry fly to the spot and stand a good chance that a nearby trout will see it and eat. If the motionless fly goes ignored longer than your patience will permit, you can always give it a small twitch. That often makes the difference.

What about a fly designed to work underwater? Yes, you can cast to the appropriate spot and just let it sink. Anglers from all disciplines know how often fish will take a lure or bait "on the drop." If you don't see fish feeding at or near the surface, let a fly descend through the water column. If it sinks about as far as it's going to and doesn't draw a strike, you can begin applying manipulation to get the attention of fish in the vicinity. Twitch it, swim it, crawl it slowly along.

If tenkara's limited casting distance is a problem on a stream, it's a bigger problem on a pond. After all, with a little wading, you can reach all or most of a modest trout stream and many spots on larger streams, provided the water is wadeable. You're not going to cast to the other side of even a small pond.

Then again, you can't do that with a fly rod, either, except on the tiniest of ponds. You often can't even get close to the middle. But you don't need to. Fish the water you can reach.

CHAPTER 6

Tenkara Fishing Techniques

I n general, tenkara fishing isn't much different than fly fishing. There is, however, an authentic style of tenkara fishing practiced by experts in Japan, and increasingly in the US and elsewhere. These tenkara-specific techniques are worth knowing. They were developed for the long rod and light line that characterize tenkara.

Kebari Manipulation

For me, this is one of the coolest things about tenkara. "Manipulation," as it's used here, basically means "jigging" in shallow water, in a very particular way. The concept of making your fly hop or dart through the water is not foreign to fly fishing, but the tenkara approach is quite different from what I was used to.

When fishing flies that work underwater, like wet flies, nymphs, and streamers, fly fishers often impart erratic action to give the impression of a bug or minnow in distress: fleeing a predator or experiencing some kind of problem or injury. They'll twitch quickly, then pull slowly, then let it drift. The idea is that the vulnerability of the bug or fish will trigger the trout's impulse to feed. It's a perfectly sensible theory that has fooled countless fish.

The Japanese method is rhythmic, methodic, and predictable—the opposite of erratic. You cast a *kebari* to the upstream end of your target water and let it sink a few inches as it begins to drift downstream. Then, with very small movements of

A tenkara traditionalist, Adam Klagsbrun employs "*sasoi*," or fly manipulation, in most of his fishing. Very slight movements of the rod and line cause the fly to hop rhythmically in the water, provoking strikes. MORGAN LYLE

Daniel Galhardo fishes pockets on the far side of Boulder Creek. By holding his line off the water, he can reach right over fast currents that would sweep a fly line downstream. MORGAN LYLE

your rod tip, you cause the fly to rise up a few inches, then drop back down, then rise up again and drop back down again. The fly does a little dance, a strange and provocative behavior that gets a trout's attention.

The movements are even and equal. The classic technique seems to be to jig the fly four times, but I'll sometimes do five or six if the fly is continuing to drift through potentially productive water. Once you've had your four or six manipulations, you lift the fly from the water and do it again.

The predictability of the movement is key. "You're looking for a rhythmic pulse that the

fish can almost time in on," says John Pearson in one of Discover Tenkara's excellent "Tenkara in Focus" YouTube videos. "If you just shake things erratically, you will get slashes at your fly, it may attract fish, but your number of hookups is drastically reduced."

Jason Klass, author of the *Tenkara Talk* blog, explains it this way:

This technique is very easy, but also very easy to botch. The key is to be subtle. You don't want to move the rod too much. When done correctly, an observer wouldn't even notice you're moving the rod. The fly should only be moving about one to three inches (not 12 inches). If you move the fly too much it not only looks unnatural, but it makes it too difficult for the fish to catch. You want to offer them an enticing but easy meal.

I'm not sure why this method works, but it does. I fish this way when I come to a pool or a deep run with a moderate current, a spot that's likely to hold fish, but with no sign of surface feeding activity. I don't catch fish every time, but I do often enough to have confidence in the technique. There could be a biological basis to it; real nymphs often do hop up and down in the water, striving for the surface, giving up and dropping back, then trying again. Manipulating *kebari* in the classic tenkara style could be considered an imitation of this behavior.

Or it may simply be that the rising and falling *kebari* gets the trout's attention. Stuff goes drifting by in trout streams all the time, bits of leaves, natural stream debris. A manipulated fly is very obviously something different.

Exactly how to move your rod tip to create this movement of the *kebari* is something you need to work out for yourself, with a little trial and error. It also varies with the nature of the water and the fly. I can tell you the movements are very small. There's probably a mathematical formula for it, but I'm the last person who would know that. I do know that when holding a 12-foot tenkara rod at a 45-degree angle, if I flex my wrist upward so that my forefinger rises about an inch, the rod tip rises about a foot. That's in my apartment, with no line attached; in a fishing situation, the flex of the rod would somewhat reduce the distance the rod tip travels. Sometimes, you can make the rod tip move

enough simply by squeezing and then easing your grip on the rod handle. The point is, don't overdo the movement of the rod tip. You don't want your *kebari* darting too far, or even worse, flying out of the water altogether.

Pools used to bore me except when trout were rising to a hatch. Even then, the trout had played half the game for me, by revealing their positions with their rises. Manipulating *kebari* gives me a fun way to try to goad fish into biting at those times when trout aren't rising (which is more often the case). It's a lot more fun than watching a bobber while a nymph drifts slowly along, unseen, at the bottom of the pool. It's also an efficient way to cover water—give a spot two or three manipulated drifts, then take a few steps downstream and try a new spot.

Whatever the reason, manipulating *kebari* is an effective technique. If it wasn't, modern Japanese tenkara experts wouldn't have spent so much time perfecting it.

Keep Your Line Out of the Water

One of the biggest advantages of level-line tenkara is the light weight of the casting line. It's less likely to cause drag or scare fish. Because of that, for a long time, I didn't worry much about letting the last few feet of line lie on the water or even fall below the surface. I did catch fish. But in recent years, some of the more active and authoritative tenkara anglers, including Gaskell and Pearson at Discover Tenkara, ERiK Ostrander, John Vetterli and Rob Worthing at TenkaraGuides LLC, and Tenkara Bum Chris Stewart, have convinced me that I will catch more fish if I make sure to keep the whole casting line off and out of the water.

Apparently, even the seemingly innocuous tip end of a lightweight level line is intrusive enough to give trout pause. There is no real way to compare Technique A to Technique B in fishing because one of the actors in the experiment is a wild animal, but the experts agreed: Once they started being careful not to let that line touch the water, they started catching more fish than they used to. That's as close to proof as you can get.

As long as you cast angling down to the water and stop your forward cast in fishing position, holding the line off the water is pretty easy to do. If you lay your line on the water and then try to pick it up off the surface, you'll lose time, and the act of lifting the line will draw the fly back toward you; it will cost you some distance.

There may be times where you have no choice but to lay your line on the water, such as when casting to a fish or a likely lie that you can only reach by ending your cast with the rod and line perpendicular to the surface so as to get the maximum distance. A situation like this is fresh in my mind as I write; two nights ago, the only way I could reach a great spot on Esopus Creek was to slap my whole line flat on the water. It worked; I hooked a decent trout that leapt and fought hard. But because I had worked myself into a crevice between sharply angled boulders the size of dining room tables at the edge of the deep pool, I couldn't back out and move downstream quickly enough to play the fish properly, and it wriggled free of the hook.

Had I held the line off the water, I wouldn't have been able to reach that trout. You gotta do what you gotta do. But if you can help it, try not to let the fish see anything but the tippet—and as little of that as possible.

Fly First

This has become a mantra among tenkara fishers. It means to cast so that the fly lands on the water before any of the tippet. The benefit of doing that may be obvious: You want the trout to see your fly, but not the monofilament it's tied to. Why is that important? It's not that trout will realize their fly is "tied" to an angler, or anything else; the concept is far beyond a trout's ability to reason. It's that the trout has spent its life eating insects that did not have a piece of nylon or fluorocarbon monofilament attached to them, and may be a little uneasy at the sight of it. The more plastic on the water, the greater the unease.

Fly-first casting also trains you to deliver your fly well and take advantage of the characteristics of tenkara. The light, relatively short line and long, sensitive rod give you the ability to drop the fly very precisely—and very gently. Several experts recommend you actually aim for a spot a few inches above the place on the water where you want your fly to land. If you've stopped your forward cast with the rod still high—11 o'clock, let's say—the line should angle down directly to the water. You are fishing the instant your fly touches down. As your fly sinks and drifts downstream, you will be directly connected, with no slack in your line to mask strikes or spoil hook sets.

The Bow-and-Arrow Cast

In case you didn't know, there are college courses in fly fishing. The best known is at Pennsylvania State University, and the best-known instructor is Joe Humphreys, himself a Penn State grad who taught the course for nineteen years. The course even has its own endowment in Humphreys's name. Humphreys is a big deal in the fly-fishing world for many reasons. He appears here because he is the guy most associated with the bow-and-arrow cast.

This isn't actually a cast, but rather a trick that makes casting unnecessary. You point the rod at the water, take the line in your hand, and pull backward to put a bend in the rod, then let it fly. The rod flings your line and fly where they need to go. You don't need to try to make a backcast, which can be a big help when a fishy spot is hemmed in by trees and brush.

This is not considered an "authentic" tenkara technique, but it does work really well with tenkara rods. It works best when the line is no longer than the length of the rod, or even a little shorter. You hold the fly itself, by the bend of the hook, and let it go as you would when firing a slingshot. (Make sure the point of the hook, and the barb if there is one, are clear of your fingers before you let go. You will regret it if they're not.)

All you need to use the bow-and-arrow cast is an opening in the brush a few feet wide. It does a good job of launching your fly in a place where it would otherwise be impossible to cast.

Of course, you may then catch a fish, and with all that brush around, you may have a heck of a time playing and landing it. Give some thought to this: It may be impossible to get that fish to your hand, especially if you want to release it unharmed. It may be better to move on to a spot that's more fishing friendly.

Hooking, Playing, and Landing Fish

You've got your gear, you're in the right spot at the right time, and you've made your cast. Here's what happens next.

Pay attention to the structure of the water. Watch for hints like the splashes of trout feeding at the surface. Flick your fly into the most likely lies first, then thoroughly cover the rest of the water you can reach. At some point, a trout is going to grab your fly.

You'll know this one of two ways: by feel or by sight. You may feel a sudden tug on your line, or you may see your line stop drifting with the current or even dart slightly in a different direction. To capture your trout, at the moment this happens you need to drive the hook into its jaw. Sometimes the trout do this for you; they have a way of turning and diving for the bottom after grabbing a fly, and if that fly happens to be tied to a line, this action will often set the hook. But generally, you'll do your part, too, with a simple lift of the rod tip. You may very well do this instinctively. Sometimes the process will fail, and you'll feel a tug but the trout will get away. That's fishing. For the most part, if a fish takes your fly, the hook will be set one way or another, and the fight will be on.

It begins with what Hemingway called "the deathless thrill of the plunge of the rod." Your trout will try frantically to escape the strange sensation of being pulled in the water. You will be connected to a wild animal, and feel its wild strength, in a way that is available to almost no one but anglers. It is thrilling in a visceral, fundamental way. I will always remember what my three-year-old daughter exclaimed when she felt a trout on the end of her line at a local fishing derby sponsored by the state conservation department: "I can feel it!"

A panicked trout will try to dash off to safety. If you are fishing with a reel, the trout can pull line behind it as it "runs." As a tenkara angler, you won't have a reel. But you do have a very long and

very flexible rod that will bend deeply, absorbing the fish's darting and lunging. A fly fisher will let the fish pull line off the reel when it runs, then reel back in when the fish relents, and can control how hard it is to pull the line by adjusting the reel's drag. As a tenkara angler, you can't do much but keep the rod up, control the fish with sideways pressure, and hope everything holds.

Everything usually does hold. The trout will pretty quickly give up its futile attempt to escape, at which point you'll be able to bring it in. Even after ten years of tenkara fishing, it still feels strange to me to do almost nothing to fight a fish except to keep the rod upright and let the fish pull against it. But that is basically all you can do, and often all you need to do.

You do have some options if you find yourself fighting an especially determined fish. You can hold the rod to your left or your right, depending which way the fish is running, to "turn" it and interrupt the run, keeping it nearby. You can lower the rod tip on one side or the other, so that the rod is parallel with the surface of the water and the pull of the fish is horizontal rather than vertical, which sometimes seems to ease the fish's panic.

If you have a strong fish and it decides to flee downstream with the current, you may need to go with it to keep the fish from escaping the hook or breaking your tippet. Chances are the fish will pause after that initial downstream dash and you can regain control.

Tenkara gear lends itself nicely to the bow-and-arrow cast, which lets you snap a fly onto the water even if there's no room around you to make a cast. Hold the fly by the bend of the hook so it won't snag your finger when you let it fly. JESSICA LYLE

How easy it is to move downstream depends entirely on where you are. You'll have the least trouble if you're on an unobstructed bank. If you're standing in shallow water that doesn't have a lot of protruding rocks or sunken logs, it's not hard to travel a few yards. If you're among a row of boulders like I was on the Esopus, you have your work cut out for you.

You must keep your rod up—or more accurately, keep it bent. Allowing a fly rod to be pulled by the fish down toward horizontal is not a problem, because the fish can pull line from the reel. With a tenkara rod, it's game over. There is no flex in a horizontal rod, and the fish will break the tippet. Trust me on this. Whether you have the rod held upright or off to one side or the other, keep it flexed. It is essential for staying in control of the fish and tiring it enough to be landed.

At some point you will sense that the fight is nearing its end. The fish will have stopped pulling, and will seem to be trying to figure out what to do next. This is when you take the initiative. Point the rod tip behind you, so that the fish is pulled toward you. Have your net ready in your other hand, and when the fish is close enough, bend down and scoop it up.

That's how it works if you're using a line that's about the length of the rod. If you're using a line that is longer than your rod, you will reach out with your non-rod hand, take the line lightly in your fingers, and pull it toward the hand holding the rod, which can then grasp it. If the fish is still too far away to reach, you may need to repeat that process to pull the fish close.

Taking a taut line into my hand seemed like a terrible idea when I started tenkara fishing, but I've done it many times since then and it

Applying sideways pressure can help subdue a strong fish determined to flee the scene. SUSAN EPSTEIN

Karin Miller taking matters into her own hands. It's often necessary to take the tenkara line in your hand when landing a fish. KARIN MILLER

Getting Snagged

Tenkara casting is highly intuitive, but there's one aspect that requires very conscious attention: the trees and brush that often grow alongside streams and ponds. It's awfully easy to get your fly stuck in this foliage. Fly fishers have the same problem. Anybody flinging a line with a fishhook on the end near trees and shrubs has this problem. You will, from time to time, get snagged. There's often nothing you can do but pull the line and hope the fly pops out intact, and you have to be prepared for the possibility that your tippet will break and your fly will remain stuck in the tree.

There's a reason tenkara fishing is so popular in Colorado and the rest of the Mountain West: Many streams in the region flow through meadows or treeless canyons, with little fly-snagging flora. You have all the room in the world behind you and need not worry about your backcast.

Where I live in New York, smaller streams in particular tend to be lined with brush, and trees often spread their leafy limbs over the water, sometimes drooping to just a few feet above the surface. This is great for trout, since it provides shade that helps keep the water cool, a prerequisite for healthy trout habitat, and often provides some treats in the form of ants and beetles that lose their footing and end up in the water. The overhead cover is also thought to make trout feel less vulnerable to predators and therefore more likely to feed actively. But it can make casting a real pain in the neck.

You can move on to another spot if things look too snaggy, or you can accept the challenge and cast carefully. Snaggy spots are often fishy spots, so if there's any possibility of getting a fly to the water, it's worth a try.

no longer troubles me. Most trout are small enough to be easily pulled in by hand, as long as you have waited until the fish was ready. Hand-lining large fish is easier than you might think. After all, if you catch a 100-pound tarpon in the Florida Keys, you're not going to reel that fish right to your perch in the bow; you will pull it close enough that your guide, amidships, can reach over the side of the boat, take the line in his or her hand and pull the fish to capture. It's all about gauging the amount of fight left in the fish. It requires a light touch; you may need to abort the process, let go of the line and let the fish struggle a bit more, then try again.

In any case, I firmly believe that playing and landing a fish on a tenkara rod is more efficient, and therefore subjects the fish to less life-threatening stress, than on a fly rod.

Don't let the prospect of losing a couple flies hold you back.

There's no fancy technique for keeping your fly out of the brush behind you. Just turn your head and watch your backcast. If you have a shorter rod with you, consider rigging it up. If the rod you're using fishes at two or three lengths, you'll naturally select the shortest one for such spots.

You can collapse one or two sections of any tenkara rod for a shorter overall length. The rod won't cast as well, but it may cast well enough to get your fly into the tastiest pocket. If you do hook a fish, try to find an opening in the foliage as soon as possible that allows you to re-extend your rod for the fight.

There's one particularly snaggy situation that you're pretty much helpless to control. It happens when your fly comes springing out of the water after something has gone wrong below the surface.

It may be that a fish you've hooked is fighting hard and the hook suddenly pops loose. Your rod will be deeply flexed during the fight, so when the fly comes loose, your rod will behave exactly as it does in a cast—it will straighten fast and hard, and fling your line in the opposite direction. That is, into the tree limbs above. The same thing can happen if your fly gets momentarily stuck on something in the water, like a branch or rock, and then suddenly comes free. Either way, you have, in effect, an unintended, uncontrollable cast straight up into snagsville.

Over time you come to expect this on some level and develop a sort of hair trigger that immediately stops this "cast," hopefully pulling the line away from danger and back to the water.

Whether you get accidentally hooked during a backcast, during a forward cast that goes a little too close to the brush on the opposite bank, or during the spring-back from a fly suddenly freed from an underwater fish or obstruction, what you do next is critical. Very few tenkara rods are broken fighting fish. Many are broken fighting snags. There's a procedure for getting unsnagged, and you must adhere to it.

Step one is to *fully* collapse the rod. Once all the sections are inside each other, step two is to take the line in your hand and pull until the fly pops loose from the snag or until the tippet breaks.

That's pretty straightforward, but it can be complicated. Sometimes you won't be able to collapse the rod, in which case you have to move closer to the snag, gaining slack and collapsing the rod as you go. If that just means walking a few steps up or downstream, it's usually no problem. If the snag is clear across the stream and you can't (or don't want to) wade toward the opposite bank, you may be left with no choice but to point the extended rod directly at the snag and pull straight back until the fly pops loose or the tippet breaks. This is a last resort; it can result in stuck rod sections, or even cause the lillian to pull off the tip. Again, do what you have to do and hope for the best. Lillians can be reattached and rod sections unstuck, though not usually in the field, so it pays to have a spare rod with you when you fish.

Wading and Waders

It's not always necessary to walk into a stream to get close enough to catch trout. Sometimes you can reach the spots you want to fish from the bank. Often, however, it is necessary, and it's also part of the fun of fly fishing. Somehow, joining the fish in their element adds to the experience. It's good, enjoyable exercise,

Wading in streams is often necessary when fishing a trout stream. It's also part of the fun. SUSAN EPSTEIN

straining against the unceasing flow of the current while eyeing that little spot of calm water behind a midstream boulder, where you just know there's a trout.

Of course, it also means you need to buy and wear waders. Our supposedly uncomplicated sport becomes a little complicated once again.

Can you wade without waders? Yes, to an extent. But there are some important cautions to be aware of. For one thing, trout live in cold water, and standing bare-legged in cold water for any length of time can be pretty uncomfortable. If the water is warm enough for "wet wading," as wading without waders is called, it's probably marginal trout habitat at best.

More importantly, wading in sneakers or hiking shoes is dangerous (and barefoot is out of the question). It's incredibly easy to lose your footing and fall if you're not wearing shoes with soles designed specifically to provide traction on underwater surfaces. Falling even in shallow rocky water can cause serious injury. You don't want a broken bone, and you certainly don't want to strike your head on a rock and lose consciousness in the water.

So almost all fly fishers and tenkara fishers wear waders, usually the kind that come up to your chest. Most wear the kind known as stocking-foot waders, which have neoprene booties, over which you wear wading shoes.

Western fly fishers usually wear chest waders with wading boots, while in Japan some anglers prefer to wear lighter wading shoes and neoprene gaiters, which function like a wet suit and protect your shins in rocky creeks and thorny brush. MORGAN LYLE

The shoes are basically hiking boots with soles designed to provide underwater traction, made of materials that can be repeatedly soaked and dried without damage.

Waders of generations past were god-awful things made of rubberized canvas, heavy, clumsy, and uncomfortable. In the 1980s, most anglers wore waders made of neoprene, which was form-fitting and lighter but which also feel clammy and clingy. Modern waders are made of light, breathable waterproof fabric, and they're remarkably comfortable in any kind of weather. If the water is really cold you can layer up a bit underneath them and be perfectly warm and dry.

So using waders is very pleasant. Paying for them and lugging them around, a little less so, but that's where we're at. A decent set of waders can be had for under $150, with another $100

for the boots. It's a chunk of change, but the investment should last for years. You can pay considerably more, and you do get what you pay for—the more expensive ones can be expected to last longer, and some even have zippers down the front, which makes them easier to get in and out of, not to mention the obvious benefit when nature calls.

Less popular with trout fishers are boot-foot waders, which don't have neoprene booties that require separate shoes. Instead, they're essentially chest-high boots. They are widely used for duck hunting or beach fishing for saltwater fish. Made of the same breathable fabric, boot-foot waders are very warm, they're very easy to put on and take off, and they spare you the expense of buying both waders and wading shoes. But the rubber boots provide less support to your feet than lace-up wading shoes, and most trout fishers prefer that support when walking in rocky streambeds.

Wading Japanese-Style

An exotic alternative to waders—at least to my Western eyes—is gaiters. They are popular with some tenkara fishers in Japan and a few in the United States. Unlike waders, they're not designed to keep you dry; they work like a diver's wet suit, which is not in fact waterproof, but still keeps you warm and comfortable. The snug-fitting neoprene only admits a thin layer of water that is immediately warmed by your own body heat. Gaiters are little wet suits that come to the knee or just above. Some have neoprene booties like stocking-foot waders, and some also have a knee pad built in for when you're crouching on the gravel to keep from being seen by the trout.

As with stocking-foot waders, you wear wading shoes with gaiters. Hisao Ishigaki wears gaiters over his waders to protect the waterproof fabric from rocks and thorns, but most anglers wear them over bare legs with a pair of shorts, or over quick-drying hiking pants.

Gaiters can be a good option in moderate to warm weather, and when fishing small streams, where often you're not even in the water and you get wet only incidentally as you work your way along. You have to accept that your feet and lower legs will be wet, although comfortably so. Above the gaiters, you'll just be plain wet. With chest waders, you stay perfectly dry (assuming they haven't sprung any leaks) all the way to your chest, but since so much trout fishing takes place in shallow streams, there aren't that many occasions to wade that deeply anyway.

One reason I stick with chest waders is that they make me virtually tick-proof all the way to my armpits. Tick-borne disease is no joke.

CHAPTER 7

The Tenkara Guru of Greenwich Village

There are plenty of places to buy American brands of tenkara rods, but if you want to buy the kind of rod that a Japanese tenkara angler would use, you will probably shop at TenkaraBum.com.

Christopher Stewart has been importing rods made by Japanese companies, warehousing them in the tiny New York City apartment he shares with his wife, and shipping them to customers in all fifty states and many other countries, since 2011. His website is a trove of hundreds of pages of tenkara knowledge, consisting mainly of detailed descriptions of each rod he sells that dwarf the one-paragraph write-ups by every other tenkara brand (and fly-rod brand, for that matter). The site is decidedly unfancy, with an early-Internet-age feel, and is utterly devoid of marketing hyperbole and gonzo buzzwords. It is friendly and encouraging, and I have never heard of anyone who doubted its credibility.

Chris is soft-spoken, polite, and considerate, with a folksy quality that belies his background as a Wall Street trader with an MBA from Harvard. The lunch he packs for a day of fishing is a ham-and-cheese sandwich on white bread in a ziplock bag. A resident of the West Village neighborhood of Manhattan, he was born in Longmont, Colorado, and grew up fishing cold Rocky Mountain trout streams with his father.

Chris Stewart, founder of TenkaraBum.com, one of the earliest influencers in the American tenkara movement. Stewart's retail business is the top American source for tenkara gear made by Japanese companies for the Japanese domestic market.
MORGAN LYLE

Daniel Galhardo was first to bring tenkara to market in America, and he had the wherewithal and resources to produce professional videos and run ads in the fishing press. Stewart has barely spent anything on advertising, apart from the occasional ad on a tenkara website and one print ad in *Fly Fisherman* magazine, but he has been vastly influential in the education of Americans about tenkara. Like Galhardo, he has visited Japan and fished with the masters, and written in detail about the world of Japanese rods, lines, and techniques. Not only did he welcome the idea of fishing for species other than trout, he did it himself, posting pictures of chunky largemouth bass caught on his annual vacations in Maine or striped bass on the flats of Massachusetts, taken with saltwater flies on a 21-foot rod designed for bait fishing for carp. He is solely responsible for the fact that you can find a man fishing for crappie and catfish in a Missouri pond with a rod called the Nissin Air Stage Fujiryu.

Chris Stewart's first fishing memory is of the annual Huck Finn Day parade in Longmont, which concluded with a fishing derby in a pond that held bluegill, crappie, bass, and, on Huck Finn Day, stocked trout. "We fished with cane poles," he recalled. "I still have mine." As his boyhood unfolded, he fished with his father, first using a bait-caster he could never master, then a spin-casting rod, then a spinning rod, and finally, when his dad thought he was ready, with a fly rod.

"It was frustrating," he said. "I couldn't see the fly, I'd get a bite and couldn't see it, and he would catch lots of fish. Mostly he fished a cast of three wet flies. I tried to fish dries, I couldn't see them and never felt the hit on wet flies. I started fishing nymphs and caught fish."

Stewart eventually got the hang of fly fishing, but as many boys do, he became interested in other things, and life went on. He took a bachelor's degree in business at the University of Colorado in Boulder, where he was more of a studier than a partier and got the grades to get into Harvard Business School.

His first job was buying and selling soybeans and corn for Continental Grain in Champaign, Illinois. He transferred to Columbus, Ohio, then to New York, where he went to work in Continental's research department. From there he worked at a firm in White Plains, just north of the city, doing research and writing reports for futures brokers. In 1983, he joined Merrill Lynch, eventually working his way up to director of commodities research. When Merrill Lynch closed that business, Chris fulfilled a longtime ambition by becoming a trader on the floor of the New York Cotton Exchange.

It didn't work out as he had hoped. He wasn't tall enough or loud enough to compete successfully on the exchange's crowded octagonal pit. "I was there for maybe close to a year before I was able to get a spot to stand where I could see," he said. "It turned out I wasn't a great trader anyway."

Or at least he wasn't a great pit trader. Stewart's next move was to rent a desk in a day-trading workspace on Wall Street. "You could buy and sell using their computers and their software, putting orders into the stock exchange," he said. "I was lucky in that I got in just as the Internet bubble was really growing, so I had a couple good years. Then the Internet bubble burst and I had a couple of horrible years, but I had done well enough in the earlier years that I never became homeless."

While all this was going on, Chris reconnected with the outdoors. He had done no fishing since going off to college; while living in the Midwest, he took up golf. In New York, he joined a club of whitewater canoeing enthusiasts, and one friend in the group was an angler, and soon he found himself trout fishing again, mainly in the stony, shady streams that ran between New York City's water-supply reservoirs among the hills of the lower Hudson Valley.

"I was a little put off by how [fly fishing] had changed since I was a teenager," he said. "It was about fancy equipment and how far can you cast and all this nonsense. My dad was never like that. He was down to earth, like 'get a rod and go fishing.' By the time I had resumed fly fishing, it was about fishing in Patagonia, fishing in Kamchatka—nobody talked about this stuff when I was a kid. You were lucky to go to the West Slope."

What got Chris interested in old-fashioned Japanese fly fishing was an old-fashioned European fly.

In the nineteenth century, trout flies in the United States and the United Kingdom got pretty fancy, with bits of feathers (often from exotic species) carefully tied to hooks to represent aquatic insects' tails, wings, and antennae, and in some cases with appendages that real insects don't actually have but that fly designers thought fish would like.

Bucking this trend were the sparse, impressionistic North Country soft-hackle flies, often nothing more than a slim body of floss or thread wrapped onto a hook shank and a feather from a partridge or starling (the "hackle") wound around the front end of the hook so that its fibers splayed out, suggesting an insect's legs. This became a full-fledged school of fly design,

first in northern England and Scotland, and then in the US.

This kind of fly suggests, rather than resembles, a real insect. Rather than flamboyant, it is understated. It has all that is needed in a trout lure, and nothing more.

"The one thing that eventually led me to tenkara was seeing a photo online of a North Country wet fly, the austere beauty of that fly, simple and obviously very effective," Chris said. "So I wanted to learn everything I could about it."

What he learned was that when such flies were first made in fourteenth-century England, they were cast with long wooden poles that had horsehair lines tied directly to loops at the rods' tips. They were known as loop rods. Reels wouldn't come into common use for another two hundred years, and yet lots of trout were caught on the fixed-line rods of the day.

"I was fishing an 8-foot bamboo rod, and I thought, 'This isn't the right rod to fish these flies.' They fished them with these long poles. OK, that's one more thing to research. So I started researching loop rods. They were using horsehair lines, so I started researching horsehair lines," which were twisted from the fibers of a horse's tail.

"I wanted to get a long rod," he said. "I thought, 'OK, I'll try a crappie pole.'"

Quick explanation in case it's needed: The term doesn't refer to the rod's quality. Crappie, also known as bream, is a species of panfish found in ponds and slow rivers across the US. A crappie pole resembles a tenkara rod in that it's telescopic and its line is affixed to the rod tip. But it's meant for tossing a bobber and a baited hook, not for casting flies.

"So I got a crappie pole, and it was awful. It was fine for what it was designed for, a bobber

and a minnow, but cast a fly? No way." He tried a 13-foot collapsible Shakespeare Wonderpole, "and it was absolutely useless."

"So I dug out my cane pole from when I was five years old, learned how to make a furled line, and went fishing. I went to the West Branch of the Croton River. It was head and shoulders better than the crappie pole. I didn't know how bad it was, because it was better than the crappie pole, but it was very stiff. But I furled [twisted] a line that was heavy enough to cast, and I was able to cast and I caught fish."

Googling horsehair lines, Stewart came across a Japanese website that mentioned their use with something called a tenkara rod.

"OK, what's tenkara? Oh my God, I don't have to make loop rod—because I don't have wood shop—and you can't buy a loop rod, but you can buy a tenkara rod. I thought, 'Aha, this is a modern loop rod, this is a loop rod that's commercially available. I can fish North Country wet flies with a horsehair line and a modern rod, fishing these flies the way they were meant to be fished.'"

The first tenkara rod the Tenkara Bum used came through the kindness of a stranger in California. In the spring of 2008, Chris posted on *Fly Fisherman* magazine's online forum, asking if anyone knew anything about tenkara. The response came quickly. "I will give you a tenkara rod," the man said. "I'm happy to help get tenkara started in the United States." It was an old, stiff, Korean-made rod that called for a heavy line. Chris found illustrations on Japanese

Using a Japanese rod designed for catching carp and a Lou Tabory Snake Fly, Chris Stewart battles a striped bass on Cape Cod. CHRIS STEWART websites that showed him how to attach a line to a lillian.

It was around this time that Chris first encountered Tenkara USA. "All through 2008, I'd do a Google search on tenkara every day, just to see what was new," Chris said. "It was all in Japanese. All of a sudden a new one popped up, in English." It was called TenkaraUSA .com. Chris sent an email and got a reply from the person who had put up the site, Daniel Galhardo. Chris emailed the site, but got no response. Several days later, another version of the site appeared, called TenkaraUSA.com, and this time Chris got a response from the person who had put up the site, Daniel Galhardo. The site was the predecessor of Galhardo's e-commerce site. The two men struck up a conversation. Chris was delighted to hear an American tenkara business would soon exist. "Hey, this is wonderful," he remembered thinking. "This way I can get a rod in the US. I didn't know how to import rods back then. I thought it was absolutely fabulous. I thought he was going to go broke," he added, doubting that many Americans would be interested. "I like it, but I'm weird."

Also in 2008, Chris made the acquaintance of Misako Ishimura, the wife of a well-known fly-fishing authority, the late Mark Romero, and herself an expert on fly fishing and tenkara. It was Misako who told Chris that Hisao Ishigaki would do a presentation on tenkara at the Catskill Fly Fishing Center and Museum the following spring.

Chris told Daniel, "You might want to come to New York and meet this guy."

Chris began building TenkaraBum.com in January 2010. The name is a nod to the book *Trout Bum* by John Gierach. Chris had zero experience in creating a website, but used the tools provided by a web hosting company in Canada.

His goal from the start was for TenkaraBum .com to be a business, and along with writing detailed reviews of the tenkara rods available for sale in the US at the time, he began selling flies, tenkara level lines cut and constructed from bright pink fluorocarbon monofilament. These particular lines were popular with some of the leading Japanese tenkara anglers, but weren't available from Tenkara USA or Fountainhead, the first two American tenkara companies. Chris had a pretty good niche.

In his pieces on TenkaraBum.com, Chris had made a convincing case for the value of high-visibility lines—how they were easier to see when the sun gets low, and how much better the angler could tell if a fish had grabbed his or her fly. The site was already becoming influential, and American tenkara fanatics began to see the kind of high-visibility line Chris sold as essential.

One day, Daniel told Chris that in order to stay competitive, Tenkara USA would begin selling this kind of line, too.

"At that point, that was the bulk of my business," Chris said. "I thought, 'My word, if he's going to cut right to the heart of my business, what can I do?' The only thing left was to start importing rods."

It was during a visit (at Daniel's urging) to the Itoshiro Fishers Holiday in Japan that Chris bought his first Japanese rod, a Shimano LLS36NB. "I really, really liked it," he said. "I thought it was much nicer than the Tenkara USA rods or the Fountainhead rods."

Chris Stewart's decision to begin reselling Japanese rods ended his friendship with Daniel. It also began Tenkara Bum's rise to prominence in the American tenkara world. No one has ever come close to bringing as many genuine Japanese rods to the American market.

Not every rod he sells is actually made in Japan. Some Japanese companies outsource their production to other Asian countries. But even these rods, Chris maintains, are superior in terms of design and quality control to those from non-Japanese companies.

"In addition to the Japanese having more of the history and institutional knowledge, the Japanese rods tend to be lighter weight," he said. "The quality is higher, the fit and finish is better. To some extent I think the Chinese mentality is similar to the American mentality: I want it cheap. The Japanese want quality. If you just pick up the rods and fish with them a while, I think you can tell the difference in just about all cases."

Chris built his business slowly, buying a few rods, seeing if they sold, buying more if they did. Each rod was described in meticulous detail on the site, which also offered many articles on Japanese fishing techniques. The site grew to include accessories and fly-tying equipment and supplies. Chris began making appearances at fly-fishing expos around the country, giving talks to Trout Unlimited chapters (as did Daniel Galhardo and other emerging leaders of the tenkara movement).

Meanwhile, Chris was on the verge of a career change. "Through several rules changes of how the markets worked, it just became harder and harder to make any money" as an individual trader, he said. So he took the plunge and made TenkaraBum.com his full-time job.

It was TenkaraBum.com that taught westerners the difference between tenkara, *keiryu*, and *seiryu* rods, and made all of them available for purchase. New rods joined the list as they were introduced, while others left as their manufacturers discontinued them. American tenkara companies, and for that matter Japanese companies, too, generally offer perhaps a half dozen rods at any given time. In 2017, Chris counted over a hundred rod models in his inventory, including different lengths and flex profiles of the same models.

Tenkara Bum Rods

A milestone occurred in 2015 when Chris introduced the Tenkara Bum 36, "the first rod developed by an American tenkara angler and a Japanese rod company for sale in America and also Japan."

Because many Americans like to fish with relatively heavy nymph flies, the rod has a slightly stiffer midsection than many tenkara models, to accommodate casting the flies and setting the hook on a fly several feet below the surface. But it is more than light and soft enough to be enjoyable when casting unweighted wet flies with very light lines in the authentic Japanese style (not to mention dry flies).

The rod is made for Chris by Suntech, a small Japanese rod maker with a very good reputation for quality. It bears the Tenkara Bum logo in the same font as on the TenkaraBum.com website, but in gold on the rod's almost imperceptibly flecked black shaft. Its handle is black EVA foam. The "36" designation means the rod is 3.6 meters long, or just under 12 feet.

The following year, Chris introduced four more rods bearing his name: 33 and 40 (3.3 and 4.0 meters) versions of the original, and, in 2017, three versions of the Tenkara Bum Traveler, a *keiryu* rod (no handle)—two that fish at three lengths and one just 2.7 meters (9 feet).

Tenkara Bum rods, made by Japanese rod company Suntech, came on the market in 2015. Chris Stewart designed the action to suit American trout anglers who fish with weighted nymph flies, as well as traditional dry flies and wet flies. MORGAN LYLE

A sideline from tenkara is Chris's spin-off business in Japanese spinning and bait-casting rods and reels. This is the kind of gear most people fish with, and some fly fishers have jokingly called it "the dark side," because it's easier and less fussy than fly fishing and therefore somehow inferior.

In fact, fishing with spinning gear can be every bit as serious as fly fishing, and the people who do it, every bit as fanatical. I remember being very impressed with the surf-casters I met when I moved from upstate New York to Long Island in 2003. They used spinning gear of the appropriate size for large, strong striped bass and bluefish. Bait-casting reels, meanwhile, are

notoriously tricky to master, and usually if you come across an angler fishing with one, you can be confident he or she knows their stuff.

Japanese reels are certainly not foreign to American bass anglers. Shimano and Daiwa rods and reels have been in common use for decades. But most of them are designed to be used for bass, other sizable freshwater fish, and saltwater species, like the surf fishing on Long Island.

Chris operates a separate website, Finesse-Fishing.com, dedicated to high-end, trout-sized, non-fly-fishing Japanese rods and reels. "You just can't buy a decent ultra-light bait-caster for trout fishing in streams. They don't exist in the US," Chris tells customers on the site.

"Truly excellent spinning rods and reels, and bait-casting rods designed specifically for trout fishing, exist in Japan."

Tenkara anglers as a group are not disappointed at catching small fish. Indeed, many would rather catch a wild 6-inch brook or cutthroat trout than a trout three times its size that had been planted in the stream by the state conservation department. Tenkara is, after all, a method that evolved for fishing small streams, and small streams hold mostly small trout.

But even most tenkara anglers wouldn't have the stomach for a strange little specialty sideline at TenkaraBum.com: *tanago* fishing, which uses essentially miniature rods and hooks to catch minnows. As Chris explains it, a *tanago* is a small Japanese fish, and the goal of *tanago* fishing—utterly perverse to almost all Western anglers, and I venture to guess to most Asian anglers too—is to catch the smallest fish you can.

It turns out there are a few Americans, mainly in the Upper Midwest, who have made a hobby of micro-fishing. The practice was the subject of a story by National Public Radio in 2016. There are a couple of Facebook groups dedicated to it. Fans are fascinated by the wide variety of tiny fish, and the exquisite beauty of some of them (if you look really close).

TenkaraBum.com carries very small telescoping rods for this fishing, as well as specialized hooks and related gear, for the handful of people who are interested. "With equipment matched to the fish, the fish doesn't have to be large to put a bend in the rod or a smile on your face," Chris says on the site.

CHAPTER 8

The Tenkara Rod

At the heart of the tenkara experience is the rod. If you're familiar with fly or spinning rods, a tenkara rod will seem strange to you because it's so long, it's so light, and it has no place to attach a reel.

You might wonder how such a wispy device could subdue a strong fish, although that will become clear the first time you catch one. You've probably never seen anything quite like a lillian, which is the small length of braided nylon attached to the rod's tip, to which the line is tied.

The fact that the rod collapses like an old-fashioned spyglass has led some westerners to look at the tenkara rod as some kind of toy. Well, it is, in the sense that all fishing rods are toys. But a tenkara rod is a serious fishing tool. It is telescopic because it has to be. If you had a line attached to the tip of a rod with ferrules, the typical male-female way of connecting sections, a strong fish could pull the top section clean off and swim away with it.

That telescopic nature also makes tenkara rods extraordinarily portable. Most of them collapse down to about 22 inches. That's small enough to pack in carry-on luggage. It takes up practically no room in a car or a home, even in a one-bedroom apartment in Brooklyn. It is far less clumsy to carry than a fly or spinning rod when trekking through dense brush and woods along the stream.

Once you've gotten the hang of it—and that usually doesn't take long—casting a tenkara rod is a delightful sensation. Small, economical movements of your arm and wrist create a smooth, responsive flex of the rod that allows you to drop your fly right where you want it. The rod's length enables you to hold the line almost

A quiver of tenkara rods. Most rods will work in most situations, within reason, but I can't help buying more anyway. MORGAN LYLE entirely off the water, above the intervening currents that bedevil fly fishers using standard PVC lines.

Twelve feet is generally considered a common length for a tenkara rod. Some are a couple feet longer, and some (not as many) are a couple feet shorter. You can also get rods that are not technically tenkara rods but work the same way that are more than 20 feet long.

A typical Western-style fly rod used for trout fishing is around 9 feet long. Spinning rods for trout, bass and other freshwater fish are usually 7 feet long or less. So it struck us as strange, to say the least, to see 12-foot rods designed to fish little streams in the woods, with the line tied to the rod tip.

The length of the rod gives you a sense of masterful control over your line and fly as you

fish. The gear is extremely sensitive, so you will know when a fish has taken your fly. Once the fish is hooked, the fight will be intense and exciting, but brief. Tenkara rods subdue fish very efficiently. Of course, the rod's prodigious flex has a limit, and the occasional fish will be strong or lucky enough to snap your tippet and get away. But you will land most of the fish you hook, and if your goal is catch-and-release, you'll return them to the water unharmed by a prolonged fight.

Let's take a closer look at a tenkara rod.

A 12-foot rod is considered the all-around size for most trout fishing. That is preposterously long by modern American and European fly-fishing standards, but it's actually a fairly moderate length in the universe of Asian fixed-line rods. For that matter, a 12-foot rod—or longer—would

Trout like this New England brown are what tenkara was made for. A fish this size will put up an exciting fight, but the rod will subdue it quickly, for efficient release. MORGAN LYLE

Take off the cap at the bottom of the handle to remove the rod sections for cleaning or drying (or replacement). MORGAN LYLE

have been very common in the U.K. before reels became commonplace in the 1700s.

Starting at the butt end of our 12-footer, the rod has a handle, much like the handle on a fly rod but usually longer. The handle is made either of cork or EVA foam. Some handles are simply a straight 12-inch cylinder; others have a shape built in, with the most common design being a bit wider on the front and back ends and narrower in the middle. This gives the angler options for where and how to hold the rod.

At the butt of the rod is a twist-off cap. Unscrewing this cap allows you to remove all of the sections of the rod. Why would you want to do that? There are two main reasons. One is that disassembling the sections allows you to dry them after a day's fishing, which will protect

their finish in the long run. The other is that if you break a section, you can easily and inexpensively replace it.

Inside this butt section of the rod are all the other sections, nesting inside each other. A typical 12-footer has eight or nine of them, all tapered. As mentioned before, the telescoping nature of the rod is necessary. The two, three, or four sections of a fly rod are joined by ferrules, where most commonly the tip of the lower section fits inside the section above. The line is never pulling on these rod sections; it runs alongside the rod, held there by guides, to the reel. If a fish pulls the line, it's pulling against the reel and the guides, not the rod. When a fish is hooked onto a tenkara line, it is pulling against the rod tip itself, and it is completely possible that the fish could pull a section joined by ferrules off the rod. The butt end of a section of a tenkara rod is wider than the tip end of the section below it, and so cannot be pulled through.

Tenkara-Rod Action

The length, taper, and wall thickness of the rod determine its action—how stiff it is, and how and where it flexes. These things are not standardized, but there is a two-digit rating system used by some tenkara companies to describe a rod's flex.

A 5:5 rod would flex evenly throughout its length, meaning it was what is called in fly fishing a "slow" or "soft" action. It lends itself to a slower, gentler casting stroke. It would feel the least stiff of the four actions. You feel the line "loading," or causing the rod to flex, more with a 5:5 rod than with stiffer rods. It is what we often call a "sweet" feel.

A 6:4 rod would flex more in the upper two-thirds of the rod. A 7:3 would do most of its flexing in the upper one-third. An 8:2 rod would flex almost entirely near the tip. The stiffer a rod is, the more vigorously you need to snap it back and forth to move the line. In fly fishing, a faster rod action creates higher line speed, which allows you to make longer casts. That's kind of true with tenkara, too, although you're seldom making what anyone would call a long cast anyway. If a 5:5 rod is "sweet," the 6:4 and 7:3 rods are "crisp." Their stiffness also comes into play in your fishing; if you are using flies designed to sink well below the surface, a stiffer rod will do a better job of setting the hook when a fish takes your fly. Stiffer rods can also exert more pressure on larger fish.

The X:X rating system is useful to an extent, and some tenkara-rod brands still employ it. But Tenkara USA discontinued using it after only a few years, finding it too imprecise to be of much value. Today, the company puts more emphasis on the length of a rod it is describing. If you'll be fishing narrow streams with lots of trees and brush near the water, a shorter rod will bump on the flora less often. If you're fishing more wide-open streams, a longer rod will give you more distance, as well as leverage to fight larger fish.

The action of a tenkara rod is in the hand of the holder. It's a subjective thing. The more advanced tenkara anglers, having spent many hours casting, will develop an idea of the kind of rod that feels best to them and suits their fishing, and will shop accordingly. But most of the tenkara rods on the market today, apart from the truly cheapo stuff, are very nice to fish with. You will adjust very easily to the nature of your rod; you'll intuitively learn how hard and how swiftly to flex your wrist to fling the line and fly where they need to go.

Rod Length and Weight

When tenkara rods became available in the United States, American anglers were as surprised by their length as they were about the fact that the rods came without reels. An old cliché of twentieth-century outdoor magazines was to call fly fishing "the long rod," as opposed to spinning rods around 6 feet long. The standard fly rod was 9 feet long, and longer ones were only used for specialties such as fishing for seagoing salmon and ocean fish.

We'll discuss this more in the section on techniques, but the long rod enables a method of fishing with flies that's fundamentally different from most fly fishing. The fly fisher casts a relatively thick line onto the water; the fly is attached to a section of thin, clear line at the casting line's end. It works quite well, but it does have its disadvantages. A fly line lying on the water is subject to being tugged by currents between the angler and the fish. It makes for a less direct connection to the fly. And often it makes fish nervous or even scares them away altogether.

The tenkara fisher uses an extremely light line, and uses the rod's length to hold it off the water, so that only the fly and a few inches of clear line are in or on the water. It avoids the intervening currents and doesn't spook fish.

Twelve feet is the length of a "standard" tenkara rod; some are as short as 10 feet and some stretch out to more than 14 feet. A fly rod of that length would feel really heavy. But tenkara rods are as light as they are long. The best ones feel like almost nothing in your hand. A typical fly rod weighs 4 or 5 ounces, and its reel adds about as much again. The best Japanese tenkara rods weigh a little over 2 ounces. Weight does not tell the whole story; some rods feel heavier than others despite having the same weight in ounces or grams, due to their design. But even the heaviest tenkara rod is really light.

Multi-Length (Zoom) Rods

There are also rods designed to be fished at two or three different lengths. In fact, theoretically, you could modify the length of any tenkara rod by changing the number of rod sections you extend. But a partially extended tenkara rod doesn't have the same action or strength of the fully extended rod. You wouldn't want to fish with it.

Zoom rods actually do work by being partially un-extended, but they're engineered to fish like rods that are fully deployed. My Daiwa Kiyose 43M fishes at two positions: 14 feet 1 inch when all nine of its 19.5-inch sections are extended, and 12 feet 7 inches when one section is left inside the handle section. When I want the maximum length, to cast farther or for the extra leverage to fight a bigger fish, I'll pull out all nine sections. When 12 feet 7 inches is rod enough, I give the second-to-last section a gentle push and slide it down inside the handle section.

The versatility you get with a rod that can be fished at two or three lengths is obvious. The Kiyose's extra almost foot and a half can be a big help when fishing larger streams, like Esopus Creek in New York or the Farmington River in Connecticut.

Zoom rods sometimes make me wonder why I would ever buy a tenkara rod that fishes at only one length. For a few more bucks and another half-ounce of weight, I could effectively own two or three rods. I guess the reason to buy a single-length rod is because you like the personality of that rod, plain and simple.

Some Tenkara Rods Aren't Tenkara Rods

As discussed, this book generally uses the word tenkara to refer to telescoping fixed-line rods used for fly fishing. But some of them are not in fact tenkara rods.

A tenkara rod is actually a point on a continuum of Asian fixed-line rods, designed to catch everything from minnows to big salmon and carp. Most of the rods available in the US are true tenkara rods: They have cork or foam handles, they are around 12 feet long, and they are designed for casting flies to average-size trout in mountain streams.

But the rods on either side of tenkara rods on the continuum are also used for trout fishing, and for fishing with flies for other species, like bass. A smaller, lighter kind of rod is known as a *seiryu* rod, and its original use in Japan is for catching small, silvery fish like chubs in calm, slow-flowing rivers. Some *seiryu* rods happen to be great tools for fly fishing for smaller trout, such as the native brook or cutthroat trout that live in the wildest mountain streams.

On the other side of tenkara rods are *keiryu* rods, which Japanese anglers use to fish for trout with bait, not flies. They can be 20 feet long or more, and they're designed to lob a baited hook and a tiny sinker or two into a spot that's likely to hold a trout.

We fly fishers don't use those 21-footers for anything, but the 14-footers make great fly rods. The stiffer and heavier models are ideal for big trout—those around 20 inches in length—and for other species of fish like bass and modest carp. *Keiryu* rods are especially well suited to fishing with heavy flies designed to sink and be fished deeply.

Unlike tenkara rods, *seiryu* and *keiryu* rods don't have handles. They just have a butt end that's thicker than the rest of the rod, usually around ¾-inch in diameter, and are coated with a fine non-skid finish. This is an odd thing for many American anglers to get used to, since pretty much all of our fishing rods have handles. But these no-handle rods transmit every little tap the fly experiences right to your hand. This sensitivity is a big advantage in fishing. The lack of a handle also saves on cost, and on weight.

Other than the handle, *seiryu* and *keiryu* rods work exactly like tenkara rods—telescoping design, with a short cord at the end, to which the line is tied.

The Lillian

Almost every tenkara rod, *seiryu* rod, and *keiryu* rod has a hollow strip of braided nylon about 1½-inch long, epoxied to the tip of the rod. You tie the line to it, using one of two knots, both of which are described in the chapter on rigging up.

This strip is called a lillian, which is an odd name for a piece of fishing gear. Here's where it comes from. That hollow braided nylon is known in Japan as lily yarn, though the Japanese pronunciation, because there is no L in Japanese, is "ri ri yan." Google Translate interprets "ri ri yan" as "lillian."

"Lillian is an English corruption of a Japanese corruption of an English term," Chris Stewart of Tenkara Bum said.

Most people who use a "girth hitch" to attach their lines to their rods tie an overhand knot in the lillian, to serve as a stopper for the knot to snug up against. I have knots in most of my lillians. They do have one drawback: That knot is usually too fat to fit through the neck of the rod section below the tip section. If you try to take those two sections apart, you won't be able to.

We are reminded by some experts, notably Chris, that we really should disassemble our rods at the end of a day of fishing, so the sections can dry fully. Letting them stay wet could eventually damage the finish. If you've got a knot in your lillian, you probably won't be able to properly separate the tip section and the one right below it, unless you actually untie the knot. Chris does that, although he's more likely to fish with level lines, which don't require a

The lillian, a short length of cord to which you attach the line. MORGAN LYLE

stopper knot for attaching in the first place. More on that soon.

Lillians have been known in very rare cases to pull off, a failure of the epoxy. But they are by no means a weak link in the connection to the fish. Lillians successfully land big fish all the time.

Small Fish and Big Fish

Just about every American who's taken up tenkara fishing has used his or her rod on big streams, which are more likely than small ones to hold big fish. Ed Van Put was no exception. The man who introduced him to tenkara fishing, however, was rather shocked.

"The ambassador would freak out when I said I used it on the East Branch or something," Ed said with a laugh, referring to the nearby East Branch of the Delaware River, a wide river that

is home to many large trout. "He said, 'If you catch a big fish, what are you going to do?'"

In fact, the *keiryu* rod Ed used on the East Branch and the Beaverkill River will handle a 16-inch trout just fine, as Ed proved on a few occasions. Nonetheless, a 12-foot tenkara rod is considered appropriate for trout up to the mid-teens. Anglers who expect to catch bigger trout on a regular basis often switch up to a sturdier *keiryu* rod, like Ed's Daiwa, or one of the tenkara rods made and sold specifically for bigger fish.

The average tenkara rod is not designed for lunkers. But we Americans love our lunkers. It was inevitable that we would wonder just how big a fish these tenkara rods can handle. It was also inevitable that people who live nowhere near mountain trout streams would be intrigued by tenkara equipment and want to use it to fish their local species, like bass.

The result was not an epidemic of broken rods. Despite the delicacy of their tip sections, tenkara-rod failure during a fight with a fish is actually pretty rare; far more rods are broken by clumsy handling.

Tenkara rods can handle large fish because they are so long and so supple. They flex deeply in response to the pull of the fish, and that ability of the rod to bend is what keeps the thin tippet from breaking. It's like the saying about a branch that bends in the breeze not breaking in the wind.

In my experience, most fights with fish consist of the initial struggle and a run or two, after which the fish pauses. That pause is when you lean the rod back to pull the fish in. There may be another tussle and more attempts to run, especially with bigger fish; you keep your rod up and let the fish battle the flex. Eventually you will be able to pull the fish to you.

Some fish are just too big to be landed on tenkara rods. If you hook, say, a 10-pound steelhead trout or a 3-foot northern pike on a 12-foot tenkara rod rated for 6X (3.6-pound) tippet, you had better hope the tippet breaks right away, because if it doesn't, your rod will.

This is not to say you will have to content yourself with catching 10-inch trout. Tenkara rods are surprisingly capable. The average tenkara rod can handle the average trout or bass just fine, and if you get lucky and hook a lunker, you stand a good chance of landing that, too.

Buying a Tenkara Rod

Tenkara rods are inexpensive compared to fly rods, but you should be prepared to spend between $100 and $250. You can get cheapo tenkara rods on Amazon for ridiculously low prices, but they have a junky feel. You do get what you pay for.

The original American tenkara company, Tenkara USA, has consistently offered a nice selection of nice rods for sale on its website and in a select number of fly-fishing and outdoor-gear shops around the country. TenkaraBum .com is the top importer of rods made by Japanese tenkara companies, and shopping and learning at the site is a wonderful experience.

At this writing, there are about a half-dozen other tenkara tackle companies in the US. All are small operations, and while a few have talked a few fly shops into carrying some of their rods, the vast majority of their business is done online. Zen Tenkara, Tenkara Rod Co., Badger Tenkara, Three Rivers Tenkara, Tenkara Tanuki, Dragontail Tenkara, Riverworks Tenkara, Tenkara Times (actually in the Czech Republic, not the US)—you will get a well-made rod that's enjoyable to use from any one of them.

What to buy? If most of your fishing will be trout fishing, in streams or ponds where there's some room to cast, and if most of the trout are smaller than 18 inches (and most trout are), a standard 12-footer will serve you well. If you'll be fishing larger streams, like the Arkansas River in Colorado or the Housatonic in Connecticut, something closer to 14 feet will help you reach more water and better control the larger fish you sometimes catch in the big rivers. But the 12-footer will work on those streams, too. You'll handle most of the fish with no problem, and if there's a spot you can't reach, you'll just have to wade closer to it.

If you're into bigger fish, there are rods for you. Rods designed to handle large fish have featured prominently in the Zen Tenkara and Badger Tenkara catalogs. The beefy Amago was one of Tenkara USA's original rods and is still a popular choice for everything from bass to carp. At Tenkara Bum, you can buy a carp rod called the Kiyogi, by the Japanese rod company Nissin, in 12-, 15-, 18-, and 21-foot lengths. It's rated for 16-pound line. There aren't many kinds of freshwater fish you can't land with it.

And if you're a fan of "blue line" trout—small native fish that live in tiny streams in upland regions, often in protected state or national forests, sometimes miles from any road—there are tenkara rods geared especially for you. Idaho-based Tenkara Rod Co. addressed the small-stream market with its Mini Sawtooth rod, effectively a *seiryu* rod weighing just over an ounce, reaching just 8 feet, 8 inches extended and just over a foot long when retracted.

So you really can't go wrong. If you enjoy tenkara fishing and do it a lot, you'll start to develop your own ideas about what kind of rod (ok, let's be real—rods) you want. To get started, visit a few manufacturers' websites, read what they say about the rods, check reviews and social media, and see what fits your budget. As when fishing, be informed, but also trust your hunch.

Rod-Length Chart: Metric/Imperial

Especially in the case of rods sold by Japanese companies, lengths are often given in metric, and are often abbreviated. For example, a rod might be described as 3.6 meters or 360 centimeters, and its name would include 36. (My Daiwa Kiyose 43M *keiryu* rod, for example, is 4.3 meters long at full extension.)

Here are some common rod lengths, in meters and feet:

COMMON ROD LENGTHS	
2.4m	7.9 feet
2.7m	8.9 feet
3.2m	10.5 feet
3.6m	11.8 feet
3.9m	12.8 feet
4.3m	14.1 feet

CHAPTER 9

Tenkara Casting

One time, I invited my next-door neighbor on Long Island over to try my new tenkara rod in my backyard. Like many Long Island anglers, he liked to fish the ocean and the back bays for striped bass and bluefish. In that kind of fishing, you fling your bait or lure as far out into the surf as you can. When he took the rod and managed to flick the fly only about a dozen feet away, he was perplexed. "Am I doing something wrong here?"

He was, a little bit. With some practice, you can cast a fly more than a dozen feet with a tenkara rod. But not much more. Tenkara fishing is close-range fishing; the casting and catching generally takes place within twenty feet of where you stand. That would be an all-but-useless cast on an East Coast beach, but it's long enough to catch trout all day in a trout stream, and even along the shores of a lake or pond (and near the shore is where most of the fish are anyway).

If you're used to casting with a fly rod or a spinning rod, this will seem strange; there's a tendency to think you have to cast as far as you can. Believe me, a 12-foot rod, a 12-foot line, and a 4-foot tippet will cast far enough to catch lots of trout.

Still, you don't want to just drop the fly right underneath your rod tip. There's a right way to cast a tenkara rig for maximum distance. I'll explain it here, but the basic procedure is pretty simple: Flick the line behind you to get it moving, then flick it forward so the fly lands in a likely place to find a trout. (We'll talk more about likely places in a bit.)

Tenkara lets you fish in the small pockets where trout hold position. Adam Klagsbrun connected with a trout three-quarters of the way across this patch of Colorado pocketwater. MORGAN LYLE

Because tenkara fishing is a form of fly fishing, I think it's useful to explain the casting by comparing it to casting a fly rod with a reel. This is important if you're coming to tenkara from a fly-fishing background. If you don't have any experience in fly fishing, you can disregard the "don't" and concentrate on the "do." So here are the key differences between tenkara and regular fly casting.

Go ahead, bend your wrist. Regular fly casting is done largely from the elbow and the shoulder, with the wrist mostly held straight. With a tenkara rod, you mainly use your forearm and your wrist. You just don't need as much leverage with a 2.5-ounce rod and all-but-weightless line, tippet, and fly.

The grip, maestro. Instead of holding the rod handle in your fist like a hammer, you extend your forefinger on top of the grip, like a conductor's baton. It provides control and helps prevent flicking the rod too far, especially on the backcast. Because you should be making . . .

Small movements. Fly casters are taught to cast between 10 and 2 on an imaginary clock face. The tenkara fisher's arm moves only a few inches, and the cast is more like 10 to 11. This is partly because a tenkara rod is so long; a few inches of hand travel will move the tip of the rod several feet. It's also because you're casting a relatively very short line. A fly caster will often be casting 30 or 40 feet of casting line, plus nine feet of leader and tippet. A typical tenkara line and tippet is between 12 and 18 feet long, and you simply don't need to move the rod tip very far to get a line of that length moving.

What's your angle? Regular fly fishers cast their line in a horizontal plane, parallel to of

Unlike the typical thumb-on-top grip of a fly rod, tenkara anglers usually hold their forefinger on the rod grip. SUSAN EPSTEIN

Your forward cast should stop with your arm no lower than a 45-degree angle. Stopping high gives you a longer cast, and makes you ready to fish the instant your fly touches the water. ADAM KLAGSBRUN

the water, and lay the line down on the water's surface at the end of the cast. In most tenkara casting, the line travels at a 45-degree angle to the water. Your backcast isn't just behind you, it's behind and above you. On the forward cast, your hand stops high and the line unrolls down to the water's surface. Ideally, the fly and tippet reach the water, but the casting line never does.

We'll discuss some exceptions to this kind of casting, but this is the basic drill. Once you've made your cast, your rod and line will form a triangle: The base is the surface of the water, one side is your upward-angled rod, and the other side is the downward-angled line.

This gives you a couple of distinct advantages. One is that because your line is held off the water, it is not subject to being pulled by the currents between where you're standing and where your fly is. That's called drag, and it tugs your fly off course. Fly fishers spend a lot of time and effort trying to avoid it.

The other advantage is that you enjoy a very tight connection to your fly. You can easily control its movement, and if a fish grabs it, you'll see or feel it instantly.

Flex the Rod, Fling the Line

If you haven't cast a fly rod before, you need to know a little about flexing a rod. Despite what I said about holding the handle like a conductor's baton, the fact is that you don't wave a rod like a conductor waves a baton. You give it a smart snap and a firm stop, in a way that will make it bend. Common and useful analogies often taught to beginning fly fishers include these: Imagine you're holding a paintbrush full of paint, and you want to make like Jackson Pollock and fling the paint at your canvas. Or imagine you're holding a stick with an apple stuck on its tip, and you want to throw the apple. Same thing—a smart snap, followed by a firm stop.

The paintbrush analogy is more accurate. Think about the bristles on the brush: As you snap the handle forward, the bristles are pulled along with it. The bottoms of the bristles move with your hand, but the tips are still catching up, so they're bent rearward. When you make the firm stop, the bristles finally catch up—they snap forward and fling the paint. This is exactly how it works with a rod. When you stop your cast, the rod tip catches up and then snaps forward, flinging the line out over the water. This flexing of the rod is what propels the line. (This is equally true in regular fly fishing and tenkara fishing.)

It doesn't take much force to produce this flinging effect. The biggest single flaw in most fly fishers' casting is using too much power. You need to cast with authority, but also with a light touch. A tenkara rod, even one on the stiff side, flexes quite readily, and that flex is what provides the energy that throws the line where you need it to go.

The Backcast

If you're not a fly fisher, you may have wondered why they cast their lines back and forth. They do this because they are casting the line, not the

The long reach and light line of tenkara fishing lets you sneak up on those small pockets where trout hide. A short, quick cast is all it takes to explore these nooks and crannies. ADAM KLAGSBRUN

Notice how Daniel Galhardo keeps his arm close to his body when casting. That's what the Japanese masters teach, to avoid fatigue. MORGAN LYLE

lure. In "regular" (non-fly) fishing, you use the rod to throw the bait or lure where you want it to go, but in fly fishing (and tenkara fishing), the lure is an almost weightless artificial fly and it's too light to throw. So you fling the line instead, and it pulls the fly and a few feet of fine, clear leader out to the target.

In fact, I consider the fact that you throw the line to be the defining aspect of fly fishing (and I'm considering tenkara a version of fly fishing here). In every other kind of fishing with a rod, the rod is used to throw the bait or lure. Only in fly fishing is the rod used to throw the line, with the lure just going along for the ride.

Throwing the line makes it possible to use extremely lightweight lures. These lightweight flies are extremely effective in suggesting the insects and other critters that fish eat, so being able to cast them is a big advantage.

To throw a line, you need to fling it behind you to get it moving, then fling it the other way to deliver the fly. That fling behind you is known as a backcast, and it is fundamental to throwing a fly with a fly-fishing or tenkara rod. The important thing to know is that the backcast must be executed with exactly the same amount of force and authority as the forward cast. Your backcast is not "getting ready" for the forward cast; it's the same thing, in the opposite direction. It's what creates the flex in your rod that propels the line forward to your target water.

One backcast is all that's needed to flex the rod. But you may find yourself doing it several times, as much to get the aim right as anything else. Maybe on your forward cast, you see that your line and fly aren't headed quite where you want them to go. So instead of letting the fly fall to the water, you go ahead and make another backcast, and this time slightly change the direction of the forward cast so your fly heads toward its target.

Your backcast should fling your line rearward just as straight and true as you want your forward cast to do. Turn your head and watch. If there's a big curve in the line behind you, you probably need to backcast with a little more force and make a more abrupt stop. It's not uncommon for anglers to think the forward cast counts more than the backcast, but with a little practice, you'll understand why both matter equally, and you'll cast accordingly.

Your line will cast straighter if you make sure your hand, wrist, and forearm travel in a straight line—on the backcast, and then on the forward cast. A slight change of direction as we discussed a moment ago is OK, but as a general rule, make your backcast directly opposite of your forward cast. This is much easier in tenkara fishing than in regular fly fishing because you're using a short line. In fact, once you've practiced a little bit—and I mean maybe an hour, or maybe even a few minutes—the tenkara backcast and forward cast become intuitive. You won't need to think about them. Your casting hand will snap the rod back and then forward without any conscious effort.

This, I think, is one of the things that makes tenkara fishing so effective. Once you're no longer thinking about casting properly, you find yourself concentrating on where your fly needs to be and what it needs to do once it gets there.

Casting at a 45-Degree Angle

I really like the angled casting that's called for in most tenkara fishing. It's not always required; if you fish with a floating line, for example, you will probably want to make your back and forward casts in a horizontal plane and lay the line down on the water, as in regular fly fishing. But most of my tenkara fishing is done in level-line style, and the angled cast is ideal.

For one thing, it helps me avoid the ever-present snags of trees and brush on the bank. A backcast that is angled upward doesn't travel as far behind you as one that is cast horizontally. If there is brush behind me that's as tall as me, my backcast will be well above it.

It's also a little easier to watch a backcast that angles up and back than one that goes straight back. Seeing the backcast helps you keep your fly out of the brush—and it also helps you make sure the cast is straight and extends fully, since those are the prerequisites for a good forward cast.

Finally, the angled cast shoots your fly straight into the water, and ends with your rod in fishing position. You don't waste a second. If a fish grabs your fly the instant it hits the water—and that happens quite often—you are ready to set the hook. If not, you are instantly in the perfect position to let a weighted nymph drop to fishing depth, or to begin manipulating a shallow-sunken wet fly to attract a strike.

Sidearm and Backhand Casting

I much prefer to fish streams where the water is flowing from my left to my right as I stand facing the stream. That's because I'm right-handed. I

This New England brown trout took a dry fly. Tenkara permits a light touch and a drag-free float that's great for dry-fly fishing. MORGAN LYLE

can stand in the stream near its edge and face at an upstream angle; my right arm is over the water and I have some room behind me for my backcast. Sometimes I have no choice but to fish where the water is flowing from my right to my left. And more often than not, there are a bunch of trees and brush that would interfere with trying to make a backcast with my right arm.

In that case, I'm often doing sort of a backhand cast, not much different from how a tennis player makes a backhand shot. My "forward" cast is going behind me to my left, and what would be the backcast is now the one that delivers the fly. It's a little awkward for me, even having done it for years, but sometimes there's

no choice and you do the best you can. Often enough, it works out just fine.

So far we've been talking about what's known as overhead casting, where your rod is generally upright throughout the back and forward casts. But there will be times when you'll need to cast sidearm.

Say there's a tree on the other side of the creek that overhangs the water, and you suspect there's a trout under the tree. They love places like that. You may even see the trout rising to snatch insects from the surface. If you try to cast down into this spot, the tree will be in your way. So you lower your rod, perhaps so low as to be parallel to the surface of the water, and cast in a horizontal plane instead of a vertical one.

I find sidearm casting to be easier than over-head casting, probably because it's so easy for me to watch the backcast alongside of me than behind me.

Of course, you will often end up with some or most of your line lying on the water, since your forward cast is stopping with the rod tip only a few feet above the surface. That takes away the big tenkara advantage of being able to hold the line off the water. It's not ideal, but if fishing a tasty spot requires you to lay your line on the water, it's a no-brainer. Sling your fly in there.

The sidearm cast is also a blessing when it's *you* that's underneath an overhanging tree. An overhead cast is out of the question, naturally, but you may be able to lower your rod and make the whole cast horizontally underneath the overhanging foliage. Again, you'll be working counter to the dogma that says your line must be held off the water, but it's all about adapting to the conditions. Do what you must to get the fly where it needs to be.

What You Lose, and What You Gain

Don't worry about remembering every word you just read. If you're like most of us, you'll be doing everything just described without even thinking about it within an hour or two. The intuitive nature of tenkara is one of its biggest advantages.

Casting at a downward angle and stopping the cast high puts your fly in fishing position the moment it touches the water. Daniel Galhardo was able to fish the small pocket on the far right of this photo by making a fly-first, fishing-position cast. MORGAN LYLE

Adam Klagsbrun making a backhand cast, and finishing in fishing position. Sometimes you need to make your backcast behind your other shoulder. It's not difficult. MORGAN LYLE

It's true, however, that experienced fly fishers who try tenkara may experience a certain feeling of loss. Or at least I did. I missed fly casting. Casting a fly line really is a fun thing to do. I have always thought it should be an Olympic sport. To do it really well takes years of determined practice.

For general fishing, it's tricky to learn, but well within reach of most people. Once the muscle memory is established, it's a very satisfying thing to feel the weight of a fly line respond to your actions, to flex a fly rod in just such a way that 40 feet of line goes looping gracefully out ahead of you above the water, to tug the line while casting so that yards of slack go zipping through your guides as if self-propelled.

You don't get any of that when tenkara fishing.

But you don't need it to catch fish, assuming you can get within 20 or 30 feet of them. In fact, in many cases, you're better off without it.

A PVC fly line is an effective tool for delivering a leader and fly to a distant spot. But when it comes to getting a good drift, controlling your fly, detecting strikes, or fishing at depth, the fly line fights you the whole time. You're continuously trying to compensate for it. You have to flip it backward ("mending") to keep it from racing ahead of the fly and spoiling your drift. You need copious amounts of weight to sink your fly quickly from the floating position of the end of the line. The line lying on the water will absorb and obscure many of the little tugs that signal a trout has grabbed the fly. If you want to jig or shake or dart the fly, you have to jig, shake, or dart the whole floating fly line first.

Tenkara fishing eliminates all these distractions and handicaps.

But the difference is even more fundamental than that. Tenkara fishing reorganizes the angler's mind. The part of your consciousness that had been assigned to casting has now been reassigned to fishing. Your arm and hand snap the rod almost automatically to deliver the fly. What you're now thinking about is where you want the fly to be and what you want it to do once it gets there. Your concentration is now entirely on the behavior of your fly on or in the water, and how it will appear to the trout.

If you come to tenkara fishing with no fly-fishing background, your mind won't need reorganizing and you won't miss fly casting. You're ready to go.

CHAPTER 10

Colorado

Bona fide tenkara fishing for trout can be found from California to Maine, and you can use a tenkara rod to fish for other species in every state in the country. But if there's one state where tenkara seems most at home, it's Colorado.

Starting at the Front Range, where the Rockies abruptly rise from the plains, and continuing across the mountainous western half of the state, rivers tumble through Colorado's canyons and ravines. Most provide fine habitat for trout, and tenkara is an ideal way to fish them, flicking casts into pockets and drifting flies down runs and glides where fish lie in wait for whatever the rivers bring them.

Huge tracts of public land provide enough access for a lifetime of adventures and discoveries. There are high-gradient mountain streams foaming with white-water, slow streams snaking across big-sky meadows ringed with peaks, and truly big, national-scale rivers—the Colorado and Arkansas are born here and have reached impressive proportions by the time they cross into neighboring states.

Many of the streams can be easily reached from roads, but many others require a walk into the wilderness, and tenkara's compactness is ideal for trekking the back country.

Most of this applies to all the states of the Mountain West. Colorado has the advantage (at least it's an advantage if you're a visitor) of being the most easily accessible from other parts of the country. Fly into Denver International Airport and you're minutes away from sublime stream fishing. For an easterner like me, driving to the rivers is part of the fun, swiveling my head from one postcard vista to another while trying to stay in my lane.

The Blue River in Silverthorne, Colorado. MORGAN LYLE

Adam Klagsbrun using a Yuzo Sebata furled line. It's sweet to cast, and easy to see in the evening light.
MORGAN LYLE

In Boulder, once you've crawled through the boomtown rush-hour traffic, it's a few thousand feet from the city streets to a canyon straight out of a Road Runner cartoon. Close to town, on a summer day, people gather in great numbers to swim and tube, but upstream, the people using the pull-offs are climbers and anglers. At the bottom, there's only enough room between the canyon's granite walls for the winding two-lane road and Boulder Creek, where Adam Klagsbrun and I picked our way upstream through pool after pool. Sometimes we cast to where a fish had shown itself, and other times we just cast to likely water.

We both used simple *kebari*, with tannish gray bodies and mousy hackles, tied on black nickel-plated size 12 Fulling Mill barbless hooks with long spears and sharp points. Between us, we caught about ten fish in an hour and a half, lovely wild browns around eight inches long. We'd have caught more, but we mostly fished one at a time, with the other guy taking pictures.

Each pool held trout. In the evening, as the canyon cooled from the day's bright Colorado sunshine, a few mayflies hatched—Pale Morning Duns? I'm not up on my western hatches— while reddish brown adult mayfly "spinners" danced around us in their aerial mating ritual.

Being good tenkara anglers, we paid zero attention to trying to imitate either the hatching or mating mayflies. But we couldn't help but notice that our *kebari* would have been a pretty good match, had we been so inclined.

Even with a hundred thousand ultra-outdoorsy Boulderites just down the road, Boulder Creek had plenty of room for fishing, at least on a weekday evening.

It had been a hot summer in Colorado. Many of the un-dammed streams had gotten so warm that the state Parks and Wildlife Department asked anglers to restrict their fishing to the morning, after the streams had cooled off overnight, to avoid inadvertently killing trout they released. No such worries on Boulder Creek. A few miles upstream of where we fished, the river had been dammed in 1909 to form Barker Reservoir, and the water released from the base of the dam is nice and cold.

Even so, Adam wore his wet wading gear: an old pair of Simms Rip Rap wading shoes ("the new ones are too stiff") and neoprene gaiters below quick-drying shorts. He fished a high-end Daiwa tenkara rod with a line made by Japanese tenkara master Yuzo Sebata, the retired Tokyo restaurateur who helped popularize adventurous, waterfall-climbing, backcountry trout fishing in Japan.

The Sebata line is furled; it's not monofilament level line. It droops significantly from the rod tip, as opposed to a level line, which angles straight down into the water. Adam bounced the sagging line with almost imperceptible movements of his hand, and the bouncing of the line translated to small rhythmic movements of the fly on the water that trout evidently couldn't resist.

A wild Boulder Creek brown trout. MORGAN LYLE

I used the line I'd been using most of the season: a tapered nylon line, the Tenkara Midi, made by the Japanese line company Fujino. The line was attached to a rod that meant a lot to me: My new Tenkara Bum 40, a beautifully appointed 13-footer that feels wonderful in the hand, casts with uncanny accuracy, and stands up bravely to big fish.

It was my second TenBum rod. I had loved my first, and had ruined it through shameful negligence. I had just finished fishing one of my local streams, the East Branch of the Croton River, forty miles north of New York City. I hiked back to the car and did what I had done many times before—lay the collapsed rod down at the base of the windshield, near the driver's side wiper. I put it there because if I laid it on the hood, it would have rolled off. Of course I would remember to bring it in the car before driving off.

I went to the back of the car, opened the hatch, stowed my fishing pack, removed my waders and shoes, closed the hatch, walked around and climbed in the driver's seat, having in the course of five minutes completely forgotten to bring the TenBum 36 inside. I never thought about it again until I was zooming down I-684 in four lanes of 70 mph traffic. The rod jostled free and flew off to its doom.

I punished myself for two years. Eventually Tenkara Bum had the TenBum 40 on sale for a great price. I have taken care of it ever since like I've cared for no other rod before.

The trout of Boulder Creek, at least where we fished, were wild browns about eight inches long. They were right where you expect them

Tenkara lets you explore a stream's nooks and crannies. Sure enough, there was willing trout in that secluded pocket. ADAM KLAGSBRUN

Downtown Silverthorne: the Blue River runs through it. SUSAN EPSTEIN

to be. We approached each pool from downstream, casting first to its shallow tail and working our way up to the head, methodically targeting water with any depth and the little passageways around midstream boulders.

Sometimes we'd see one rise and try to catch it, which sometimes worked and sometimes did not. Some fish rewarded our guesswork. In a couple cases, having worked our way to the head of the pool, we turned around and cast to the water we had just fished—but instead of letting our flies sink, we skittered them across the surface so that they made a wake. It's a Japanese tactic called *tomezuri*, and we caught a couple that way, too.

Adam and I covered a couple hundred yards of the creek that evening. We could have gone

on for miles, but it was getting dark, so we packed it in.

Rainbows the Retail

An hour west of the Front Range, a really good trout stream exists in an improbable setting. The Blue River winds through the three shopping centers that make up the outlets at Silverthorne. Sue and I didn't decide to spend a few days in Silverthorne because of the river or the outlets, though we availed ourselves of both while we were there.

I did get a kick out of the fact that as the Blue River flows past Banana Republic and the Gap, its riffles and pools hold enough big trout for the river to be classified by Colorado Parks and

Wildlife as a Gold Medal stream. Colorado confers Gold Medal status to a publicly accessible stream that holds at least sixty pounds of trout, with at least twelve of them 14 inches long, per acre. A little over three hundred miles of the state's nine thousand miles of trout streams hold the designation.

Of course, the outlets is just a tiny stretch of a river that flows about fifty miles, from the uplands behind Breckenridge to its confluence with the Colorado River at Kremmling. North of Silverthorne, the Blue flows through the Colorado countryside, and while access is spotty, it affords the normal rural trout-fishing experience.

But that part of the river lost its Gold Medal status in 2016. Now, in its first forty miles, only the three-mile stretch of the Blue River downstream of Dillon Dam is considered Gold Medal water. That's the stretch that includes the outlets.

The reason why the best part of the Blue is among the shopping center is eighty-foot-deep Dillon Lake, an impoundment just upstream of Silverthorne. Like Boulder Creek and so many other trout rivers in the US, the Blue River comes flowing out of the dam that forms the lake really cold. Trout thrive in cold water.

Trout also love shrimp, and the water coming out of Dillon Dam happens to have plenty of it. The state planted the tiny species known as Mysis shrimp in the reservoir in the 1970s as a source of food for the kokanee salmon that had been stocked there. The shrimp turned out to be more of a boon for trout downstream of the reservoir than the salmon behind the dam. As on a couple of other Colorado tailwaters, the Frying Pan and Taylor Rivers, the Blue below Dillon Dam holds some trout that are way bigger

than you would expect to find in a stream of its size. Experts credit the shrimp diet.

I guess you could think of all this in a way that doesn't sound terribly inviting: fishing next to a shopping center for a non-native fish species (rainbow trout, imported from the West Coast) feeding on non-native forage (the shrimp) in a river kept artificially cold by a big reservoir.

But, hey, there's some nice trout in there. And I did find a couple of good buys in the Columbia store.

Fortunately, Silverthorne's city fathers left a buffer of trees along most of the river, even in the densest part of the business district, so you're not actually looking at dumpsters and loading docks while you fish.

Sue and I rented a second-floor apartment in a suburban house just north of the business district, with a postcard view of Red and Buffalo Mountains out the picture window. Behind the homes on the other side of the street was the paved bike path that runs alongside the river in town. I had the exquisite pleasure of having coffee from the Airbnb's Keurig while gazing at the mountains, then putting on my waders and boots on the landing of the outdoor staircase and walking to the river to fish.

The Blue is wide and shallow, although not as shallow as it looks. There are so few well-defined pools that the local authorities and conservation groups built rock dams and installed boulders to create some structure for the fish to live near. Trout like big rocks because they break the current, giving the fish a place to sit comfortably while awaiting aquatic bugs on the current. Anglers like big rocks because it gives them some idea of where to cast.

That first morning, shivering in just a T-shirt and cheap hoodie (dressed for muggy New York

Semi-urban trout fishing in Silverthorne. SUSAN EPSTEIN

instead of bracing Colorado), I waded up the left bank, the shady side, and patiently swam a *kebari* through every run and alongside every rock I could reach, with no success.

There were no really deep holes, but there were plenty of spots for fish to hide. I concluded they were present but not yet active, having spent the night in that cold Dillon Lake water. There was no reason for the trout to be out and about, anyway; I saw no aquatic insects on or above the stream for the fish to feed on. The bugs were probably cold, too.

Finally, I came to something resembling a pool. It was probably two or three feet deep, and its surface was wrinkly, not glassy. It was actually pretty nice habitat. Don't ask me why, but I decided to put away the *kebari* and switch to a dry fly: a size 12 ant pattern, made of foam with a couple turns of black hackle in the middle,

and some bright orange on its back so I could watch it float more easily.

This little inspiration paid off with the only trout of the morning. A nice rainbow, bigger than the fish I'm accustomed to back East, calmly rose and took the ant from the surface of the water.

Being a decent-size fish—14 inches, maybe 16—it put a nice bend in the TenBum 40. But it really didn't fight that hard, and rather quickly allowed me to pull it to my feet. In fact, the hook pulled loose when I had the trout in front of me, but the fish didn't take off and allowed me to scoop it up in my *tamo* net anyway. Not his first rodeo maybe.

Back home, looking at maps on the computer, I began to question whether I was actually allowed to fish where I had been. If I was reading it right, that water was private property, which may have explained why no one else was fishing. Of course, it was a Thursday morning,

A paved bike path provides easy access to the Blue River. MORGAN LYLE

The South Platte River in Eleven Mile Canyon. The canyon offers superb trout habitat amid postcard-worthy scenery, with ample access for fishing. MORGAN LYLE

and the local anglers were probably on their way to work. In any case, I didn't see any signs.

I fished again in the afternoon, farther upstream, closer to the business district. This time I found a long, shaded pool with lots of good cover, several rising trout and mayflies on the wing. Despite the fact that trout occasionally fed at the surface, I tied on a *kebari* instead of a dry fly. I swung the fly over deep spots, near rocks, and anywhere a trout had shown itself, and ended up catching half a dozen fish, all rainbows well over a foot long. Unlike the lazy anteater, they fought hard and leapt, and felt ice cold and muscular when I reached into the net to release them.

The next day, it was back to dry flies, this time all the way up among the outlets. A series of man-made boulder dams created pools roughly fifty feet square. Each one had nice deepish water where the river spilled over from the pool above, and long tongues of current. But fishy as the water was, I couldn't buy a bite. Sometimes, fish in spots like this choose their battles. At dusk, the pools may have come alive.

Gazing upstream, however, I saw fish rising in the uppermost pool.

I hiked up the right edge and found it easy to get into position. The water flowed from my right to my left. I was maybe ten feet upstream of the boulder dam, the deepest part of the pool, where the water picked up momentum before tumbling over the rocks. The current was too swift for the trout to sit in and wait for food. These fish hid among the boulders in the

Some people say rainbow trout are easy to catch. I prefer to think of them as cooperative. This one took a dry fly on the Blue River in Colorado. MORGAN LYLE

dam itself. When a fly came drifting down the quickening current, a trout would dart from the rocks and snatch it off the surface before it was lost to the pool below.

A number of times the fly that came drifting down was a Deer Hair Emerger dry fly, tied to Sue's line or mine. The trout did their jobs, and we enjoyed some time on their pool, barely noticing the hum of commerce in the background.

Eleven Miles of Trout

It was Sue's idea, bless her heart, to go visit Eleven Mile Canyon before we returned to New York. We had been there once before and fallen in love with the canyon's beauty and good trout fishing.

The South Platte River cut this cleft in the granite after crossing the meadows of South Park—not the fictional town where Stan, Kyle, Kenny, and Eric live, but a broad plain of ranch land about an hour's drive northwest of Colorado Springs. Like so many of the rest of the great rivers in Colorado and elsewhere, the South Platte is kept cold by releases from dams. At least four major reservoirs have interrupted the river by the time it reaches Denver: Antero, Spinney, Eleven Mile, and Cheesman. In the cold water below each of them, the trout fishing is superb.

Three sections of the South Platte are on Colorado's Gold Medal rivers list. Eleven Mile

Canyon isn't one of them, but it doesn't matter. Everyone who cares about Colorado trout fishing knows about it and loves it. The canyon is in a recreation area owned by the US Forest Service. You pay seven dollars at the guard shack at the eastern end of the canyon, just off Route 24 in the community of Lake George, and enter the canyon on a washboard dirt road alongside the river. The road, which used to be a railroad bed, bores through the rock in tunnels at three spots. There are a few picnic areas and campgrounds, but the area is otherwise undeveloped—no shopping centers here. In spots, the pink/gray canyon towers straight up, but in other places the angle is gentler and the walls are forested with ponderosa pine.

Access to the water couldn't be easier. It's right next to the road. The water itself is diverse in character, with everything from whitewater flumes where no fish would live to calm meadow stretches where you may catch a glimpse of a chubby trout lazing among waving underwater grasses.

Sue and I found a pool with moderate current hidden from the canyon road by head-tall brush. We saw only the occasional mayfly, and by looking, you couldn't be sure there were any fish in the pool at all—until Sue found one.

I had jumped in first, working downstream, drifting and swinging a *kebari*, and hadn't gotten a touch. I had gotten about thirty feet when Sue called to me, and I turned around to see her rod bent double. Fishing the same water I had fished minutes before, but with a dry fly, not a *kebari*, she had watched a 16-inch rainbow appear like magic from the streambed, ascend to the surface and bite.

It was the first of three we encountered in the pool. We only landed one. Sue's trout freed itself of the hook just as I was reaching for it with my net. "Good for you," she said to the fish.

Naturally, I switched to a dry fly—Wyatt's Deer Hair Emerger—and re-fished the water I had started on. It was only a matter of a few casts before I got a nice rainbow of my own. It attacked as the fly drifted downstream over three feet of water in the center of the pool, and it did everything an acrobatic rainbow trout should do: pulled, zigzagged, and leapt, then allowed itself to be netted, briefly admired, and released.

A hefty Eleven Mile Canyon rainbow ends up in my *tamo* net. The long tenkara rod makes it easy to hold the line off the water, so that dry flies drift naturally—very important when fishing for rising trout. SUSAN EPSTEIN

107

BROKEN & REPAIRED

June 17: On Father's Day, I broke a rod. It was one of my favorites, a Tenkara Times Try 360. I got my line tangled up in some brush behind and above me and, in direct contravention of the advice I give in this book, was yanking on the line with my rod to try to pull it free. The tip section snapped.

One of the great things about tenkara rods is how easy it is to bounce back from something like this.

June 18: I sent a Facebook message to Anthony Naples, proprietor of Three Rivers Tenkara in Pittsburgh, from whom I had bought the rod. It's just that easy. I've done it a number of times.

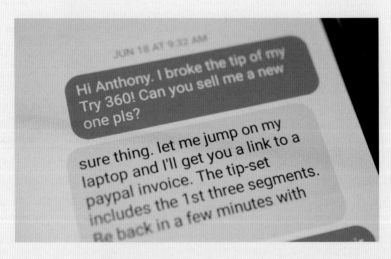

JUN 18 AT 9:32 AM

Hi Anthony. I broke the tip of my Try 360! Can you sell me a new one pls?

sure thing. let me jump on my laptop and I'll get you a link to a paypal invoice. The tip-set includes the 1st three segments. Be back in a few minutes with

June 20: My replacement tip section arrived. The top three sections, actually.

I unscrewed the cap on the butt of the rod, removed the other sections, inserted the replacements, and reassembled. Five minutes' work.

June 22: Back on the water: Esopus Creek.

Boulder Creek shimmers in the summer sun. The cold, clear trout streams of Colorado's Front Range are ideal for tenkara fishing. MORGAN LYLE

The river was maybe thirty feet wide here. Along that part of the far bank directly across from us was a smooth rock wall, about the height of a wall in a house. By wading toward midstream (after we had hooked the two fish there), I could reach the base of the wall. Because fish love structure, the wall looked like good habitat, and I floated the dry fly down right next to it, then probed it with subsurface flies. Nothing.

But at the right edge of the wall, the upstream edge, there was a cave. A hollow in the rock, three feet wide, three feet high, and just deep enough to be dark. It formed a tiny bay alongside the current. I hadn't tried to fish it yet, because to reach it, I would have had to wade into the heart of the pool. But the little cave was obviously the prized lie, the best hidey-hole

in the whole stretch of river we could see. And because we'd already pulled a couple of good trout out of the center of the pool, I didn't feel bad about marching in there to cast.

Staring at the cave as I began to make my way across the pool, I saw a mouth. Not a splash, not even a bulge, just the snout of a trout quietly piercing the surface to capture an unseen insect.

It's at moments like this when I most appreciate the precision of tenkara casting. I was using the TenBum 40, the green Fujino tapered nylon line, four feet of 5X tippet and the Deer Hair Emerger. Between the very accurate rod and the fact that I was only fishing about 16 total feet of line and tippet, I was able to drop the fly right at the upstream edge of the mouth of the cave. On the first cast, too much of the tippet was lying on the water and was grabbed by the current, dragging the fly across the cave mouth like a water-skier.

That sort of thing makes some trout so uncomfortable they quit eating for a while. Fortunately this was not one of those trout. I moved a step closer and held the line up higher on the next cast, which allowed the fly to sit nearly motionless in the calm water, and one second later, the water was calm no more. The little bay in the cave exploded so violently I wondered whether I had hooked into one of the behemoth trout you hear about out west.

I pulled the fish out of the cave and it fought me in the main pool. It wasn't a behemoth, just a mid-teens brown. As it thrashed, another fish executed two splashy rises in quick succession a few feet downstream, and I had the distinct impression it was some kind of copycat behavior. Many times, I've seen a trout rise in a pool and then the rest of the fish follow suit.

In any case, I wasn't connected to the brown trout for very long. It got below me in the current, and just as I was beginning to wonder if I should chase it downstream, the tippet snapped and the fish was gone.

The catch and the quick fight were so satisfying that I didn't even bother casting to the copycat fish. Meanwhile, a group of fly fishers with big bobbers on their lines came around the upstream bend and exhibited a poor sense of personal space by crowding into our pool. But it was time to go anyway. We had a rental car to return and an overnight flight from Denver to JFK. We packed our wet boots and waders into our empty second suitcase along the edge of the dusty dirt road and headed out of the canyon.

CHAPTER 11

A Foothold in the Appalachians

"I don't consider just dangling a leader and fly in the water to be fly fishing," a well-known fly-fishing author once told me. It was like that at the beginning for tenkara in the US. (It still is with some people.) In the first couple of years after the launch of Tenkara USA, acceptance was slow in coming.

At board meetings of the American Fly Fishing Tackle Association, "there was good-natured joshing," said Tom Sadler, the conservation lobbyist, avid fly fisher and board member. "Ridicule would be overstating it. It was joking around, like 'Hey, get a reel, hippie.' Stuff like that."

Sadler, a Rhode Island Yankee who settled in Virginia and guides people fishing for trout in the Allegheny Mountains and the Shenandoah Valley, understood the appeal of tenkara early on. He tried to convince the AFFTA's board members, mostly owners of retail fly-fishing gear and outfitting businesses, that tenkara was not a threat to their livelihoods—and could in fact increase their business. He encountered skepticism.

"There was that whole 'tenkara's a fad' thing, and 'it's not gonna be around very long,'" he said. "Jeez, what's this, you've got a piece of equipment that's inexpensive, that doesn't use a reel, that doesn't use a traditional fly line, how is that helping the business?"

But Sadler himself had been convinced by a couple of big-name outdoors entrepreneurs—Patagonia founder Yvon Chouinard and Craig Mathews, owner of Blue Ribbon Flies in West Yellowstone, Montana, the epicenter of American fly fishing—that tenkara was a legitimate method of trout fishing, and its

Tom Sadler, conservation lobbyist and fishing guide, was an early adopter of tenkara.
MORGAN LYLE

Tom Sadler's license plate makes his enthusiasm for tenkara clear. A fishing guide and conservation advocate, Sadler was one of the early American adopters of tenkara. MORGAN LYLE

inviting, nonintimidating style could draw new participants into the fly-fishing community. They would get to enjoy casting flies and catching trout without first having to take weeks of fly-casting classes and memorize a college semester's worth of obscure information.

On the contrary, he argued, tenkara could boost their business.

"If I can show [prospective anglers] a more simple approach, something they can do intuitively and that gets them out of having to learn the casting skill and really only having to learn the fishing skill, big lightbulbs go off," Sadler recalled over burgers in a trendy café in Staunton, Virginia. "Everybody gets it. And while the industry or some people within the industry might laugh at the tool, they won't laugh at the

result. And this is what Yvon Chouinard had figured out at Patagonia. . . . It was because of Yvon Chouinard and Craig Mathews that I came to tenkara. And it wasn't until after I had talked to Craig and read Yvon's piece, ironically enough, in *Fly Rod & Reel* magazine, that I glommed onto it. The first rod I bought, I bought from Craig Mathews. And I started talking about what a great thing it was, and that's when Brian and Colby approached me and said, hey, we kind of dig this tenkara, we see this tenkara thing as pretty interesting opportunity."

Brian and Colby Trow are the owners of Mossy Creek Fly Fishing, a well-appointed fly shop with a substantial and loyal clientele in a nineteenth-century brick house in Harrisonburg, Virginia. Fly rods line the shop's western wall. Wooden bins in the center of the shop are divided into dozens of little wooden compartments, each holding numerous hand-tied flies (there is no other kind) designed to catch everything from trout to smallmouth bass to striped bass to tarpon. Stacks of folded plaid shirts, Mossy Creek T-shirts and hats, fly-fishing chest packs and backpacks and sling packs and vests, and modern rain gear fill the other rooms of the house.

One room is lined with packages of the feathers, furs, tinsel and chenille, beads, and fishhooks that are used in tying one's own flies. In a room devoted to chest waders, a tailgate from a 1964 Ford F-100 pickup truck, complete with working taillights, is mounted to the wall, so anglers can sit while trying the waders on, just the way they would put them on alongside the creek on a summer morning.

The brothers Trow appreciated tenkara as a serious pursuit. "There's a lot of passion and honor in Japanese fishing," Brian said. And they grasped the similarities between mountainous Japan and mountainous Virginia, and tumbling creeks full of small, wild trout in both places. They realized tenkara was designed, had evolved, for places like the Appalachians. Unlike most of the fly-fishing establishment, they concluded that tenkara had a place on American trout streams.

So up went a modest display of Tenkara USA rods (after delicate negotiations with the company, which was exceptionally choosy about authorizing dealers). Sadler began offering guided tenkara fishing trips through the shop, to fish for wild brook trout in the mountain streams. The Trows became tenkara ambassadors. Fly fishing was still the majority of their business, but tenkara was in the mix. Within a couple of years, Mossy Creek had become a famously tenkara-friendly fly shop.

"The Original Form of Fly Fishing"

"For the first few years that we had tenkara, we felt like we were selling snake oil," Brian said. "People would come in and they were very leery of it, they had a lot of questions. They would come in sometimes three, four times, asking probing questions, and finally be like, 'OK, I think I'm going to do this now.' That was unusual."

As we chatted near the tailgate in the wader room on an unusually chilly April morning, I asked him whether he and Colby had gotten pushback for embracing tenkara.

"Big time," he said. "Big time. Daniel [Galhardo] obviously took his licks, coming into the industry not selling a reel, preaching the notion of only using one fly in an industry where we've got a billion flies and fly boxes and fly tiers. I mean, everybody took some licks.

"Some of the things that were hard for people to argue against were the benefit of getting people into the sport easier, number one, and starting youngsters earlier. I got all my kids started probably four or five years earlier than I would have had they just gone with a conventional fly rod. That was huge for me. I do a lot with Project Healing Waters, where we've been able to get a lot of folks that have limited use or no use of a limb, that's been huge. The benefits for folks like disabled veterans who really need that tool, you can't naysay that stuff. You cannot do it.

"It was a little bit harder convincing our customers that it wasn't just training wheels on a fly rod, that tenkara rods are actually superior in certain settings," he said.

The settings he referred to are mainly mountain streams. Harrisonburg sits in a valley of dairy farms, with the Allegheny Mountains a half hour to the west and the Blue Ridge Mountains a half hour to the east. It's perfectly possible to fish mountain streams with regular fly-fishing gear, but tenkara does it better. The streams are small, so tenkara's limited casting distance is not a handicap. It is simpler and therefore easier to flick little casts into every pocket, pool, and run with a tenkara rod than with a fly rod. Most of the fish are small, so there's little risk of breaking the fine tippet line used with tenkara rods.

Even if you do happen to catch one of the few lunkers hiding in every stream, it won't be able to sprint very far, and you can usually control it well enough in its little pool to bring it to hand. Not unimportantly, when it's time to move to another spot, the fact that you can collapse a tenkara rod to less than two feet long makes it easy to carry through trail-less brambles in the dense eastern forests.

And then there's Mossy Creek itself, which is not a tumbling mountain creek, but rather a placid, spring-fed stream meandering through the farmland. The fact that its water comes from underground means it's always cool, which is ideal for trout and the insects they eat. Mossy is stocked with plenty of fish, but its habitat is better than most "put-and-take" streams, and its trout tend to prosper and grow fat. Its modest width means you can reach the whole thing with a tenkara line. Mossy Creek Fly Fishing owns a stretch of the creek, and also coaches customers on where and how to fish the publicly accessible parts.

Brian and Colby Trow on the tailgate at Mossy Creek Fly Fishing in Harrisonburg, Virginia. The shop carries tenkara gear as well as fly-fishing tackle. MORGAN LYLE

Mossy Creek Fly Fishing in Harrisonburg, Virginia, was one of the first American fly shops to embrace tenkara. MORGAN LYLE

So there's lots of tenkara fishing to be done nearby.

"We knew immediately that it suited the small streams we have here really well, because it's very similar to the streams of Japan," Brian said. "The fish are similar. Everything's similar."

Mossy Creek became something of a tenkara laboratory, Brian said. He and Colby lobbied Tenkara USA to make shorter rods that wouldn't bang into the Appalachian foliage as much as the 12-footers. They asked for rods that could be fished at different lengths. They reported how often customers would lose the little plug that goes in the end of the collapsed rod when you're done fishing. Tenkara USA's Rhodo—a rod that can be fished at 8 feet, 10 inches; 9 feet,

9 inches; and 10 feet, 6 inches and has a spot to stash the rod plug so it won't get lost—is named for the rhododendron Galhardo encountered on the trout streams of North Carolina during a visit to Mossy Creek, Brian said.

Tenkara rods that can be adjusted for length were not actually a new concept, but Brian's point is well taken. Tenkara USA did indeed respond to feedback from its customers, and it was beginning to have quite a few of them in Virginia and North Carolina. Attendees at the big regional fly-fishing expos crowded the Mossy Creek installation for information.

"The shows were crazy," Brian said. "You could get like fifty people swarming your booth, all trying to hear about tenkara. They would say, 'There's not a lot of stuff that's new in fly fishing.' But I would say, 'This isn't new. It's actually really, really old.' It's insane to me how it hadn't made its way until Daniel brought it. How did it not come here earlier? I mean, it is the original form of fly fishing. People would say, 'That's not fly fishing.' I would say, 'Actually, that *is* fly fishing. That's how fly fishing was done for centuries.'"

Mossy Creek also did big business in tenkara rods online. "I wasn't just growing it in the Shenandoah Valley. I wasn't just growing it in the Appalachians," Brian said. "I was selling tenkara rods all over the United States. And those sales could have been as easy as someone just clicking a button, or they could have been as long-winded as twenty, twenty-five back-and-forth emails with a guy who had a million questions."

The Orvis Connection

The Mossy Creek crew takes credit for one of Tenkara USA's biggest breaks: a place in the most important catalog in fly fishing. It was at Mossy Creek, they say, that Tom Rosenbauer got to see how well tenkara rods fished—and how well they sold.

Rosenbauer was marketing director of the Orvis Co., easily the biggest and best-known brand of fly-fishing tackle (along with clothing, outdoor gear, and home furnishings). Founded in 1856, Orvis operates a network of brick-and-mortar stores across the country. Its catalog, in print and online, has been a fixture of fly fishing for decades.

As told by the Mossy Creek folks, Rosenbauer was in Virginia for a visit to Mossy Creek, one of its dealers, and went fishing with Colby on Ramsey's Draft in the George Washington and Jefferson National Forest. Rosenbauer worked his way up from pool to pool with a fly rod and reel, and Colby fished behind him with a Tenkara USA rod and caught lots of trout in spots where Rosenbauer had already fished and caught few or none.

Also on the weekend in question, Sadler gave a well-attended workshop on tenkara fishing, and a number of customers were impressed enough to buy a rod.

Rosenbauer's recollection of fishing with Colby on Ramsey's: "It impressed me. It was fun. Seeing sixteen rods sold in one fly shop in one afternoon also impressed me."

Whether because of what he observed on the stream or at the cash register, Rosenbauer made a decision that would be momentous for Tenkara USA: Orvis announced in July 2012 it would carry one of the company's tenkara rods in its venerable, widely read catalog and in its stores.

Tenkara USA pronounced it a "huge milestone" and "an irrefutable validation of tenkara."

At the time, Galhardo told me he and Rosenbauer had discussed such an arrangement for several months. He also said he had rebuffed offers from big-box sporting-goods chains to carry his rods because he didn't think they would present tenkara, the gear, and the Japanese-style method, properly. He trusted Orvis to take tenkara seriously.

Galhardo held the third Tenkara USA summit in Harrisonburg in 2013, drawing scores of new devotees and the curious for seminars on casting, tying flies, and fishing techniques. The same year saw the first Appalachian Tenkara Jam, then and now one of the country's biggest tenkara conclaves, in the mountains of western North Carolina. Word was getting around.

Ramsey's Draft, in the Virginia Allegheny Mountains, offers excellent tenkara fishing for wild trout in a wilderness setting. MORGAN LYLE

Also that year, Galhardo the Trows and Orvis collaborated on a documentary. The result was *Blood Knot*, a beautifully filmed, utterly engaging thirty-minute film about two handsome young twin brothers having a ball fishing for big trout, carp, and muskellunge (a big, prehistoric-looking apex fish). Most of their fishing is done with rods and reels, but tenkara is well represented, including a sequence in which Brian uses a large fly meant to imitate a mouse to entice a fat brown that any angler would have been proud to catch.

Such movies have proliferated in the past decade, to the point that there's a traveling film festival that packs venues in big cities and small towns across the country. And in a publicity coup that Mossy Creek and Tenkara USA couldn't possibly have hoped for, *Blood Knot* won Best Film of the Year at the 2014 Drake Film Awards. *The Drake* had by then become the most passionately read fly-fishing magazine in the country. Now, many of its fans had seen expert fly fishers catching trout—including big trout—with tenkara rods.

CHAPTER 12

The Tenkara Guides

ERiK (that's how he spells it) Ostrander moved from his native Texas to Salt Lake City, Utah, in 2000 because "the rock climbing was really good and the tuition was the cheapest out-of-state." He was already a fly fisherman when he learned about the newly launched Tenkara USA late one night while browsing fly-fishing forums online. It was cheap and intriguing. "I thought, hey, I might as well try this and see what it's all about," he recalled.

"It showed up, and I went up to my local stream and just *destroyed* it," ERiK said, by which he meant the tackle worked very well. "I caught so many fish. I averaged a fish every three minutes. It was just so fast. I came home after fishing that day and I packed my bags and left for a trip to Panama for ten days, and the whole time I was in Panama I was thinking about coming back and fishing tenkara. For me, what appealed to me was how efficient it was. It was just so good at fishing mountain streams."

This is a common story among the fly fishers who gave tenkara a try when it arrived in America. It was cool, it was affordable, and it worked really well.

In the summer of 2009, only weeks after tenkara was sprung on the western world, ERiK met another tenkara fan from Utah—seven hundred miles from Salt Lake.

In Los Angeles on business, ERiK posted on Tenkara USA's forum, asking whether anyone in the area wanted to meet up and fish. Answering the post was John Vetterli, who had grown up in Park City, Utah, and retired after twenty-two years with the Park City Fire Department. John had moved to LA for a second

Rob Worthing, ERiK Ostrander, and John Vetterli (l–r) founded Tenkara Guides LLC in Utah in 2011. JOHN VETTERLI

career as a commercial helicopter pilot, giving tours and pointing out movie stars' homes below. He saw ERiK's post and took him to Azusa Creek Canyon in the San Gabriel Mountains, just east of the city.

"Beautiful stream," ERiK said. "It's an urban stream, so you turn one corner and there's a couch, and you turn another corner and there's underwear. So we found a couch, women's undies and trout."

Vetterli was a tenkara angler waiting to happen. He had nurtured a lifelong interest in Japanese culture, starting with karate lessons in 1975 at age twelve, and eventually to include *laido*, the art of drawing and cutting with a samurai sword; Zen Buddhism; *kendo*, or Japanese fencing; and the elaborate and meticulously prescribed practice of the Japanese tea ceremony.

At the same time, he had been a fly fisherman since his late teens. And even though he had the Provo River nearby, a substantial stream with lots of big trout, he was drawn to the smaller streams in the mountains.

A month after his trip to Azusa Canyon with ERiK, John was back in Utah for a visit, and the two of them convened a small meeting of tenkara enthusiasts. Daniel Galhardo came all the way from San Francisco to meet them. Also in attendance: Rob Worthing, a former navy medical doctor on a yearlong sabbatical from the University of Utah, who had stumbled upon tenkara while looking for lightweight fishing gear for backpacking. (One of the earliest

John Vetterli works his way, pool by pool, up a small stream in Utah. John has established strong ties with the Japanese tenkara community, and shares what he has learned with students in the US. JOHN VETTERLI

Rob Worthing stalks a pool on a wilderness stream, using a boulder for cover. ROBERT WORTHING

endorsements of Tenkara USA came from *Backpacking Light* magazine founder Ryan Jordan, who produced complimentary articles and videos about tenkara fishing for food and for sport in the backcountry of Montana.)

The three of them fished the Provo for a couple of days before John returned to his aviation work in California. He wouldn't be there much longer. "About six months later, I was sitting in gridlocked traffic on the 210 freeway, counting the days until I could move back," he said. "I called ERiK on the phone and said, 'Hey what do you think about starting a guide company?'"

"The rest of that summer ERiK and Rob and I kind of figured out how to be fishing guides, because none of us had ever done that before," he said. "We found a bunch of intrepid friends to practice on. It was a year of marathon fishing. It was fish-on-the-brain crazy."

ERiK estimated the three of them spent a total of three hundred days that first year tenkara fishing on Utah trout streams. ERiK, John, and Rob officially launched Tenkara Guides LLC the following summer, on August 1, 2011.

There are lots of fly-fishing guides, but there aren't many that know how tenkara works. Back then there were none at all. Tenkara Guides LLC described itself as the first fixed-line fishing guide company in the Western Hemisphere. Veteran fly fishers and people who had never fished at all signed up to learn how to use the long, willowy rods on the sparkling streams of the Mountain West.

All three are public tenkara advocates, writing articles and giving talks. The company only actually runs a couple dozen guide trips a year; the guides are selective about their clients. "We want people that want to learn, that are interested in becoming better fisherpersons," Rob said. "We're not so interested in the corporate clientele that just wants a nice outing for the day."

Tenkara Wins a Tournament

A month after launching the guide service, ERiK had the audacious idea of entering what was then called the Utah Single Fly Event, a high-profile fly-fishing competition on the mighty Green River. It went better than he could have hoped.

ERiK saw that one of the four-person teams had lost a member, and volunteered to fill the spot. He showed up the night before the competition at the motel near Flaming Gorge Reservoir, where competitors were staying, and announced he wouldn't be using a fly rod, but rather a tenkara rod, a 13-foot Amago from Tenkara USA.

His teammates weren't sure this was a great idea. "The guys had me over to their room to talk strategy," said Brian Hoskisson, the guide who would be in the boat the next morning with ERiK and teammate Paul Stay. "Everyone pulls out their rod tubes, and [Ostrander] pulls out this tiny little tube and stretches out this 13½-foot thing across the room.

"I had seen them before, but I had always figured they were for small streams only, so I was kind of wondering if we weren't gonna go out there and have a rough time of it," he said. "I suggested he bring a western rod with him as a backup, but he said, 'I'm gonna give this a try.'"

The tournament, which raises money for conservation projects, attracts serious anglers, and a poor showing would have been embarrassing for ERiK, not to mention lousy PR for tenkara. But this wasn't ERiK's first time fishing the Green, and he had reason to be confident.

As the day went along, ERiK dropped his single fly—a grasshopper imitation made mainly of foam—into the Green River's pockets and eddies, luring trout after trout to the surface. At the end of the day, ERiK's team won the thirteen-team tournament. ERiK had caught thirty-three trout, more than any other angler in the contest, except one—and the one was a man named Lance Egan, one of the most famous and accomplished fly fishers in the country.

"The biggest thing that impressed me right off was how well he could fish the pockets with having minimal line on the water," said Hoskisson, who has guided on the Green for eight

ERiK Ostrander showed how effective tenkara gear can be when he helped his team win the Utah Single Fly Event competition on the Green River in Utah. ERIK OSTRANDER

The Demon and the Bum: Masami Sakakibara, known as Tenkara No Oni (Tenkara Demon) for his expertise, and Christopher Stewart, proprietor of TenkaraBum.com, at Oni School in Utah.
CHRIS STEWART

years. "The only thing touching the water was his fly. We'd go along and ERiK would just pick the pockets as we'd go."

That night, at the post-tournament banquet, "A lot of these guys told me, 'If I had known you were going to use a tenkara rod ahead of time, I would have tried to talk you out of it,'" ERiK said. "Now there are a lot of people that want to fish with me."

The Tenkara Devil

The most notable accomplishment of Tenkara Guides LLC has been bringing Masami Sakakibara—the Japanese tenkara master playfully nicknamed Tenkara No Oni, which translates into something like Tenkara Demon—to the United States. Each summer, the Guides host what has come to be known as Oni School, providing twenty students with three days of personal instruction from Oni on trout streams in the Salt Lake area. Oni is a big deal among the tenkara anglers of Japan and the US, and Oni School sells out quickly.

Well into his sixties, Oni inspired America's new tenkara anglers with his nimble rock-hopping, graceful casting, and intuitive fishing prowess. When casting a *kebari*, or trout fly, to a likely pocket in the stream, he is the picture of concentration, which earned him the demon nickname from admiring fellow anglers.

"Oni is just boom, boom," ERiK said. "The things that he can do with a fly are just so cool. Oni has got such a laser focus."

Oni was born in the mountains of Japan in 1951, learned to fish from his father, and engaged in sport fishing of every kind, including fly fishing, fishing with spinning rods, both bait and lure, and fishing the ocean shores. But his affection for tumbling mountain streams led him to make tenkara his specialty in 1976.

ERiK and John met Oni in Japan in 2013. The year before, Tenkara USA had held its second tenkara summit in Salt Lake City, and attendees from Japan included Eiji "Eddie" Yamakawa and members of the Harima Tenkara Club. John struck up a friendship, and soon came an invitation to visit Japan the following summer. A fishing trip with Oni was on the itinerary. The master hit it off with the young Americans, and eventually contacted them about teaching in the United States. After a scramble of organization, the first Oni school took place in 2015.

Rob lived in Japan for two years, but doesn't trace his affection for tenkara back to the experience. "I'm not somebody that's interested in tenkara because of a particular interest in the Japanese culture," he said. "I met a lot of people and they were excellent fishermen, and I learned something from all of them.

"But then came Oni," he said. "Masami was the first one that I met that I just couldn't believe what I was seeing. I had hit a plateau and didn't know where to go from that plateau, and then met Oni and realized there were seven dimensions parallel to the plateau that I was on that I didn't know existed."

Rob Worthing with a nice rod—a Tenkara Bum 40—and a nice trout. Worthing, a doctor who lives in Louisville, Kentucky, is a sought-after speaker and teacher of tenkara. ROBERT WORTHING

At the Oni schools, "I feel relatively confident that I can narrate what he's doing and why, and to an imperfect degree then mimic it in demonstration. But what he does is so subtle, it's not even on the radar of some fishermen, until you have it pointed out to you."

"Despite my difficulty sometimes of the idea accepting a master or sensei, if I had one, it would be Oni."

"It's so cool to see him fish and know what he's doing," ERiK said. "There are many other anglers from Japan who are good. But they don't have the same fire that Oni has."

The guide service was never a full-time business. "Tenkara guiding has never been lucrative enough that it could be our only source of income," ERiK said. All three of the guides have day jobs. Worthing has since relocated to Lexington, Kentucky, where he practices medicine and does some tenkara guiding in the Appalachians. Vetterli is a trainer for the Transportation Security Administration. ERiK's background is engineering, but he assumed stay-home-dad duties in 2018 when his daughter was born.

The guides continued to spread the word. Rob travels to give talks as his schedule permits; in 2018, he was a guest speaker at the sixth annual European Tenkara Convention in Norway. ERiK has taught a three-day intro course at the University of Utah. John has given two-hour basics classes at Robert Redford's Sundance Mountain Resort. For 2018, a second Oni school was added, and quickly sold out.

"One of the things that I've noticed is that we're getting more interest from the millennial crowd, the twenty-somethings," John said. "The die-hard fly fishermen are never really going to give this sport a chance, but younger guys and women are interested."

Tenkara Lines, Tippets, and Spools

Playing with the different kinds of lines is one of my favorite things about tenkara. There's much more variety among tenkara lines than there is in rod-and-reel fly fishing. In fact, there's more variety among tenkara lines than in the forest of tenkara rods available today. Casting a monofilament level line is a different experience from casting a braided, tapered line, and they're both different from casting a floating tenkara line.

Fly fishers do have specialized lines, like sinking lines or lines with special tapers for use with those long Spey rods, but the large majority of the time, they're using a weight-forward floating line for trout fishing. The relatively fat business end of the weight-forward line gives it some weight for casting, and it works well. It's a versatile line and a pleasure to use.

The modern Western fly line is usually a stout nylon monofilament coated in very supple PVC. It's a descendant of lines made of silk, which in turn are descendants of horsehair lines, which aren't actually a horse's hair, of course, but rather fibers from its tail.

That means the Western line and tenkara lines have a common ancestor. The original tenkara rig, until as recently as the early twentieth century, consisted of a bamboo pole and a horsehair line.

There are several kinds of tenkara lines. Here I'm using a tapered nylon line, thick enough to cast well and easily seen, but still light enough to hold off the water while hiding behind a boulder. ADAM KLAGSBRUN

The Western fly line evolved from the horse-hair age with a distinct personality. The taper changed; most people liked a line that tapered on the business end in the early twentieth century, but as the decades went along, the fat-ended weight-forward line became more popular. The lines have always come in different weights, to match rods that were used for different kinds of fish, from sharks to brook trout. But apart from the taper and the weight, for the most part, a fly line is a fly line.

Tenkara lines were a bit schizophrenic when the method was revived for recreation in the mid-1900s. Two distinct lines became popular.

The level line is just what it sounds like: a length of monofilament line of even strength and diameter. A typical example is a 12-foot length of fluorocarbon mono, in a high-visibility color so you can track it as your fly drifts. There's a Japanese classification system for these lines based on their weight, and we'll get to that shortly, but in pound-test terms, level-line tenkara fishers are typically casting 10- to 15-pound-test fluoro, with a few feet of clear, lighter tippet at the end.

The other kind of line is what American and European fly fishers might recognize as a furled, or twisted, leader. It's made of several strands of fine mono or even cloth thread that are twisted into a nicely tapered casting line. This line, too, gets a few feet of tippet on the end.

Some people like one kind, some like the other. This division in line preference is a complexity in tenkara's personality that's kind of at odds with the whole "simplicity" thing, but it's also part of the fun. I like both kinds. Each one has clear advantages and disadvantages. Since the tapered, furled line claims the title of "traditional," we'll look at that one first.

Furled Line

The great advantage of this kind of line is how sweetly it casts. If you come to tenkara fishing as an experienced fly fisher, you will immediately recognize the feel of the line "loading" the rod, traveling in a tight loop and laying out gentle and straight to the water.

If you're not experienced with fly fishing, you may find the tapered line more pleasant to use during your first few casts, because it provides tactile feedback: You can feel the line tug the rod when you fling it behind you, and you can turn that tug around to fling the line forward over the water with a smart forward cast. It becomes obvious pretty quickly how this is supposed to work, and then it's just a matter of practicing a little and tinkering with your cast until it does what you want it to do, and drops the fly where you want it to be.

The taper of a furled line is another thing that makes it easy to cast. Fly-fishing lines and leaders have always been tapered, to carry the energy of the cast down the length of the line while allowing the end of the line and the leader to land gently, rather than slapping onto the water like a clothesline. Furled tenkara lines work the same way.

Another thing I like about this kind of line is how it connects to the rod. Not only did tenkara develop two styles of line, it also developed separate ways of attaching the line to the rod. I don't think it's necessary, but there you are. I prefer the method used with the braided/twisted/furled/tapered line. At the rod end of the line, there's a little loop of fine, strong string. Fly-line "backing" is sometimes used. You use this loop to make an easy, dependable knot called the Girth Hitch that connects your line

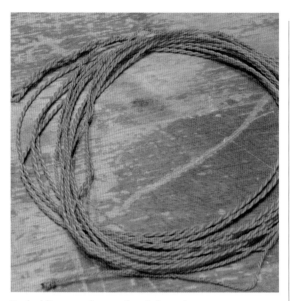

Furled line can be made of thread or monofilament. It sags a bit from the rod tip but is very pleasant to cast, and some Japanese tenkara masters use them exclusively. MORGAN LYLE

to your rod. Consult the chapter on Rigging for detailed instructions. I just find this attachment method the easiest to use.

Finally, those traditional lines are easy to see, and that's important in tenkara fishing. It's how you know where your fly is and whether a fish has grabbed it. Thin level lines can be surprisingly difficult to see, even when they're colored in high-visibility orange or pink. It often depends on the background and the time of day. This is pretty much never a problem with a braided, tapered line, due to its much larger diameter.

The big disadvantage of traditional lines is that they are heavy.

Not heavy in your hand, of course. But the twisted or furled line is heavy enough to sag from the rod tip and end up partially lying on the water.

The tapered line mimics Western fly lines both in the casting feel and in this tendency to droop from the rod tip. Level-line tenkara anglers will tell you they can fish more effectively with a line that angles straight down into the water, keeping them in touch with their fly and affording them great control over where and how it drifts.

Another complaint about many of the tapered lines is this. If you get your fly snagged on a bush on the opposite bank or a submerged log, and you pull the line to break off, the snap of the breaking tippet sometimes convulses a braided line into a tangle that takes several minutes to smooth out. It's not difficult to do; you just stroke the line back into shape. But it's a hassle no one needs while fishing.

Still, it's the sag, not the occasional twisting, that got braided tapered lines a bad rap during the establishment of tenkara in the US. We were told that being able to cast a very light line and hold it entirely off the water gave us a major tactical advantage. Relatively heavy furled lines drop onto the water, possibly scaring trout, and are susceptible to being dragged by intervening currents, spoiling your fly's natural float. The real sharpies in Japan, we were led to believe, use level lines only.

In fact, however, some of Japan's best-known tenkara masters prefer furled lines. Hiromi-chi Fuji, author of the 1990 book *Modern Tenkara*, didn't just use them, he developed the best-known furled line, the Nissin Pals. Yuzo Sebata, famous for his adventurous expeditions in rugged headwater streams, also makes and fishes his own furled lines. When Tenkara USA opened for business, it sold a green furled line labeled "traditional" along with level line.

That Tenkara USA traditional line was the first tenkara line I casted, and I loved it right away. But the idea that level lines were stealthier made sense to me. I transitioned to level lines and have mostly stayed there.

Level Line

A fly fisher who didn't know better would probably look at a level casting line and call it a leader. In fly fishing, after all, the casting line is a PVC-coated nylon cord; the only monofilament in the fly-fishing rig is the 10 feet or so of clear leader and tippet at the end.

A fly line has heft that makes casting possible, since in fly fishing you cast the line itself, not the nearly weightless fly. This is largely true in tenkara too, but in tenkara, the whole system is so much lighter and the rods have so much more flex, the relationship between the rod and the line is different.

I've seen it estimated that a 13-foot fluorocarbon level line weighs about half a gram. By comparison, the first 30 feet of a 5-weight fly-fishing line, the size often thought of as an all-around trout line, weighs 9.5 grams—twenty times as much. Thirty feet of 5-weight fly line would dramatically over-flex a standard tenkara rod. A .5-gram tenkara line wouldn't flex the average fly rod at all, and while you could flex the fly rod with exaggerated casting motions, it would do a lousy job of casting the tenkara line.

Slim, willowy tenkara rods, on the other hand, are designed to cast extremely light lines. Heavier types like furled lines "load" or flex a tenkara rod quite readily. I don't actually think

Level line is sold by the spool. It's heavy enough to be used as a casting line but light enough to be held off the water, a big advantage when presenting a fly to a wary trout. MORGAN LYLE

a level line loads a tenkara rod very much; I think most of the flexing comes from the casting motion. But the level line is heavy enough to be flung, and that's all you need to make a cast.

In fact, casting a level line is a pleasure. With an unweighted fly, the rig feels responsive and completely under your control. It's easy to direct your backcast away from obstacles behind or above you, and your forward cast is precise.

The small diameter of the level line probably makes it less frightening to fish during false casting (though you should still keep your false casting to a minimum anyway). If a little bit of the level line lands on the water, it creates barely any disturbance—far less than a furled line.

It is after you have made your cast, with your fly and tippet in or on the water, that the level line really shines. You can effortlessly hold the whole line off the water, forming that triangle with the rod as one leg, the line as the other, and the distance between you and the fish as the base. You're in direct contact with the fly. It is easy to manipulate the fly in any way you may wish, and if a fish takes the fly, your hook set can be virtually immediate. The line is unaffected by currents between you and the targeted water, so your fly won't be dragged off course.

Another nice thing about level line: It's completely customizable. It is sold by the spool, and you can cut it to whatever length you like. I usually use it a foot shorter than the length of the rod, with a 4-foot tippet attached. So with a 12-foot rod, that's 11 feet of level casting line plus 4 feet of tippet for a total 15 feet.

You can use quite a long level line (by tenkara standards) if you like. Some people routinely fish 18 or 20 feet, plus their tippet. Any capable tenkara rod can certainly cast a line of that length just fine.

But I'm trying to get into the habit of using a shorter line—maybe 2 feet shorter than the rod. For me, landing a fish with 20 feet of line on a fixed-line rod is a chaotic mess. There's an awful lot of hand-lining, which I try to keep to a minimum, and the biggest trouble is when the fish runs toward you and suddenly you have slack in your line and no way to reel it up. I would much rather use a shorter line and find a way to get closer to the water I'm targeting, or else just move on to water I can reach with a line and tippet just a little longer than the rod.

Level-Line Sizes

American and European fly fishers are quite used to using fluorocarbon as the material for their leaders. It is thought to be less visible to fish in the water. It is also denser than nylon, from which most monofilament fishing line is made, and that's why it makes a good tenkara casting line. That density makes it heavy enough to load or flex the rod a bit, and to respond to rod-flexing provided by your casting motion by stretching out behind you and in front of you to deliver the fly. It can be flung.

Because the fly-fishing and tenkara worlds, both Western and Japanese, avoid common-sense definitions at all costs, there is a nomenclature for the size of your level line. It doesn't apply to furled lines or the specialized lines we will discuss shortly. It only applies to level lines.

A line classified 4.5 is about the heaviest any trout fisherman will use, and is actually considered too heavy for many tenkara rods. A No. 4 line is thought of as the heavy end of the normal-use range, helpful when throwing big flies or on a windy day. A 3.5 might be considered the all-around line size, suited to most tenkara rods and light enough to easily be held off the water. A No. 3 line is on the lighter side, meant for use with small, unweighted flies and much easier to use when the wind is calm than when it is not. Size 2.5 is considered a finesse size, more likely to be used by skilled casters with sensitive rods, trying to catch wary trout in tricky conditions like calm, shallow water.

Here's a chart published by my friend Jason Klass, author of the best blog on tenkara, *Tenkara Talk*:

Japanese Rating	Metric Diameter	Imperial Diameter
#2	0.235 mm	0.009"
#2.5	0.260 mm	0.010"
#3	0.310 mm	0.012"
#3.5	0.3155 mm	0.0125"
#4	0.330 mm	0.013"
#4.5	0.3556 mm	0.014"
#5	0.370 mm	0.015"

There are a couple of points we can glean from this chart. One is just how fine level casting line is: generally about one-third of a millimeter, or one-hundredth of an inch. Another is how small the differences are between the line sizes. A No. 4.5 line is two thousandths of an inch fatter than a No. 3 line—yet you would feel the difference between the two when casting. That's how sensitive tenkara gear is. That's also why playing a 12-inch trout can be a pretty exciting experience with a tenkara rod.

Floating Line. This is essentially a length of light, non-tapered fly-fishing line. Daiwa, one of the top Japanese fishing-tackle brands (their spinning and spin-casting reels are quite popular in the US), sells it for the Japanese tenkara market, and most US tenkara tackle companies sell versions of their own. They have been welcomed by those tenkara anglers who come from a fly-fishing background. Daiwa even calls theirs the Floating Fly Line, acknowledging the blend of fly fishing and tenkara the line represents.

Using a floating fly line on a tenkara rod isn't a new thing: Patagonia founder Yvon Chouinard has fished that way for decades, and one of the original Japanese tenkara experts and authors, Keigu Horie, did the same.

Floating tenkara lines are heavier than level lines and can't be held off the water as well, but fly fishers are perfectly comfortable fishing lines that lie flush on the water's surface. These lines are especially useful for dry-fly fishing, and they can be used the same way on a tenkara rod—add 6 or 8 feet of tippet of the size appropriate for the dry fly you're using, and cast your fly upstream of the feeding trout. Floating tenkara lines are also excellent for casting floating poppers for bass, just like with a fly rod.

Despite their weight relative to level lines, some anglers fish them tenkara-style very successfully, including Tom Sadler in Virginia. Sadler likes to use a "dry-dropper" rig, with a sunken nymph dangling several inches deep below a floating dry fly. The floating line delivers this rig nicely, and Tom leaves only the last couple feet of line on the water, so he avoids intervening currents and enjoys a mostly direct connection to his flies.

Finally, having a line that lies on the water isn't always a bad thing. A level line held above the water's surface may be unaffected by currents, but it is highly susceptible to wind. A gust can billow the line like a sail and drag your fly off course, or even pop it out of the water

Tom Sadler of Virginia uses a floating line most of the time. He finds it effective for casting "dry dropper" rigs to the large trout of Mossy Creek in the Shenandoah Valley. MORGAN LYLE

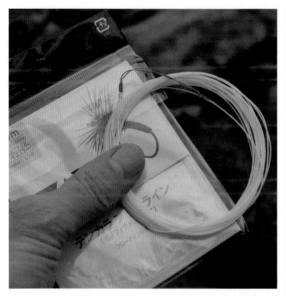

Floating line gives the tenkara angler an experience much like Western fly fishing. It's especially good when twitching popper flies for bass. MORGAN LYLE

altogether. A line lying on the water is more or less anchored there by surface tension, and while that may not be ideal, it's way better than a line blowing around in the air.

Daiwa's floating tenkara line comes in 4-, 5-, and 7-meter lengths, which equates to 13.1, 16.4, and 23 feet. American tenkara companies offer similar lengths. Since floating tenkara lines generally aren't tapered, you can always lop a little off if a given length is too much.

Alternative Tenkara Lines

There are alternatives to furled and level lines, and they're worth experimenting with. Most are relatively inexpensive (around twenty dollars). Most come with a loop on the rod end for attaching with a girth hitch; the tippet end is

135

unfinished, allowing the angler to connect the tippet in their preferred method.

Tapered Nylon. This is monofilament-like level line, but as the name suggests, it's not level, it's tapered. Tapered lines are desirable in fly fishing and tenkara for the way they "turn over" the fly, delivering it smoothly and gracefully toward the target. These lines are heavier than level lines, so they sag a bit during your drift. But they cast very nicely, and most of all, they're super visible. The company that specializes most in this style of line is Fujino.

Horsehair Line. It is possible to buy premade horsehair lines, as well as horsehair line kits. If you're enterprising, you can get a hank of horsehair sold as replacement for violin bows and make your own. It involves simply twisting a few strands together, sealing each end with a knot, then making a thinner bundle and attaching the two, continuing until you have the length and taper you desire. Instructions can be found online.

They cast nicely, but apart from that, there's no great strategic advantage to using twisted horsehair lines. They're about as heavy as furled lines made of nylon mono or cloth thread, and they're considerably more prone to breaking. I guess people mainly fool around with them because they enjoy the old-timey-ness of it.

USING A "SIGHTER"

Competition fly fishers often use very long leaders and hold them off the water, very much like tenkara fishers. The clear leaders are hard to see, so the anglers often incorporate "sighters" into them. A sighter is a foot or two of brightly colored monofilament, something you can watch as your fly is drifting downstream. If the sighter suddenly twitches or stops drifting, you'll know you may have a fish.

A sighter can be helpful to the tenkara angler for the same reason. Even orange or pink level line can be hard to see, due to its fine diameter, and the sighter provides a contrasting color to focus on.

A sighter can even allow you to use ordinary clear monofilament fishing line as your casting line. After all, level line is nothing more than 12- to 15-pound-test fluorocarbon monofilament, colored for visibility. Clear fluorocarbon monofilament will work just as well, except for the visibility part, and that's where the sighter comes in.

Even with a sighter, casting and fishing a clear level line is pretty tricky, and not worth the trouble in many cases. But a rig like this is very stealthy and is worth a try when casting to spooky fish in calm, clear water. A white sighter, as opposed to a bright-colored or multicolored one, is difficult for fish to see since it blends with the sky when looking up, especially on a cloudy day.

You can find sighter material sold as such. The original was Sunset Amnesia, which comes in spools of red or chartreuse.

Tippet

That few feet of fine, clear line between your casting line and your fly is especially important in tenkara fishing. It is what makes your fly appear to be a natural, living organism. It's also the fail-safe that protects your fragile rod tip from breaking under the strain of a large fish.

Tenkara rods are slender and light, with very thin tips. This design is necessary in order to be able to cast very light lines, and to be flexible enough to withstand being pulled by hooked fish. They're surprisingly capable, but they are far from indestructible. That's where the fail-safe tippet comes in. If you hook a fish that's simply too big to land, the tippet will break before the rod does.

But it works both ways: The rod protects the tippet, too. Even fighting a modest fish, a tippet may break if attached to a very stiff rod, but will hold when the rod itself can flex. You can use very thin tippets, which catch more fish because they are less obtrusive.

How thin? If you're an experienced fly fisher, nothing heavier than 5X for trout fishing and 4X on the stouter rods for bass.

If you're not an experienced fly fisher and are wondering what 5X means, I have some more arcane terminology for you. I'll try to be brief.

The "X" system of rating tippet dates back to a time when natural thread, extruded as goo by cultivated silkworms, was drawn through successively smaller holes to reduce its diameter enough to be used as a fine fishing tippet. A rating of 5X, for example, meant the "gut" had been drawn five times.

Today, extruding machinery can make nylon or fluorocarbon tippet any size that's required, but the old nomenclature remains. Just to make things more confusing, the larger the X number, the lighter the tippet. The standard trout-fishing tippet is 5X, which (coincidentally) has a breaking strength of about 5 pounds, but sometimes it's necessary to use finer tippet, such as 7X, which breaks at about 2.5 pounds. If you think you might catch really big trout, you might opt for 3X (6 pounds).

Here is what all that X stuff means in practice. If you will be trout fishing, use 5X tippet. If you want a less-obvious tippet that will probably catch more fish, and you don't mind losing a fish once in a while, use 6X.

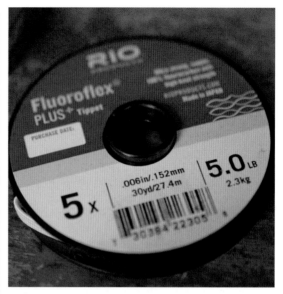

Rio is a popular brand of tippet, the fine, clear line at the end of your casting line, to which your fly is tied. Like level line, it is sold by the spool.
MORGAN LYLE

You may even want to consider using 6X as your default tippet. In fly fishing, 6X is getting down into the ultra-light category, but it's stronger on a tenkara rod, because the rod is so much more flexible than a fly rod. You can always switch up to 5X or even 4X if you have reason to think you might be catching big fish.

Some Japanese rod makers, but not all, specify the heaviest tippet that should be used with their rods. Few American tenkara-rod companies do.

Line Holders

We tenkara people don't use reels, but we do use spools—to keep our lines stored neatly when they're not in use. There are all kinds, from small, rustic bamboo racks to simple foam discs with grooved edges.

The classic tenkara line holder is a blue, 2-inch hard plastic spool with a yellow foam core and a hole at the center. When you're ready to move from one spot to the next, you collapse your rod, hook the fly to the spool, wind your tippet and line onto it, then poke the rod through the hole in the center of the spool and let the spool slide down onto the rod.

You don't have to use a store-bought line holder. Early on, frugal tenkara anglers discovered that a slice of a foam pool noodle would work just about as well. You can carve a groove for the line if you want to get fancy. On the opposite end, some tenkara gear companies and individual craftsmen sell beautiful, hand-carved

wooden spools, some with separate grooves so you can store multiple lines.

At this writing, Nissin and Tenkara USA make fancier versions of line holders, and they're really nice. The Tenkara USA model is well crafted of sturdy plastic, has a little metal bar you can hook the bend of your fly over, and holds two lines, with a tough, rubbery guard over the groove to prevent them from unwinding in transit. It even has a tiny fly box built into the center of the spool, near the hold for the rod. You really could put a few nymph flies in there and carry nothing more than the holder and a spool of tippet when you fish.

Line holders aren't just for temporary storage when moving from one fishing spot to another. They're also great for permanently storing

A sampling of tenkara line holders: the classic blue Meiho line holder with a foam core, fancier models by Tenkara USA and Nissin, and a simple model made of black foam. MORGAN LYLE

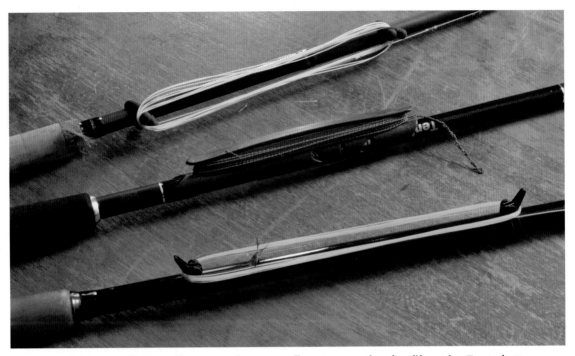

Having something to wind your line onto when you collapse your rod makes life easier. Top to bottom: cable-tie line holders, Snap-On Line Winder, EZ Keepers. MORGAN LYLE

lines. They are, however, a bit bulky. Taking up less space are the Diichi-Seiko Spool Sheets, paper-thin discs with little tabs that hold the line, along with spaces where you can jot down the line's size and length, and lots of cool Japanese writing.

Of course you can always coil-up a line on your fingers and slip it back into the cellophane sleeve it came in or a fly fisherman's leader wallet.

On-Rod Line Storage

We're getting perilously close to a reel here. Having a way to wind your line onto your collapsed rod saves you the trouble of retrieving a line holder, winding on the line, then stowing the holder again when you resume fishing. Of course, you could simply wind the line around the handle of your rod, like Matt Sment does. Matt prefers the simplicity of not needing an extra piece of equipment. But it takes a lot of wraps to wrap a line around an inch-thick rod handle, and just as many to unwrap it.

Early on in the American tenkara years, Jason Klass, founder of the indispensable *Tenkara Talk* blog, hit on a great idea. There's a product meant for use on spinning rods that are not fitted with hook keepers—a little loop near the handle where you can hook your lure to keep it secure when not fishing. The product is called the EZ Keepers, and it's a little plastic tab that sticks up from the rod, held in place by a rubber O-ring wrapped around the shaft. Jason figured

139

Originally sold as hook keepers for spinning rods that didn't have them built-in, a pair of EZ Keepers makes a great way to store line on a collapsed rod while moving from one spot to the next. MORGAN LYLE

out that if you put two of these on your rod, one leaning rearward, the other leaning forward, you could leave your line attached to the tip of your collapsed rod and wind it around the two EZ Keepers.

Genius. Most tenkara fishers tried this, and many of us have stuck with it. You can add a third O-ring on the rod to slip the point of your fly under. It really is quicker and easier than winding the line onto a separate line holder.

Other versions of on-rod line storage emerged over time. Tenkara USA introduced something called Tenkara Rod Ties, a short length of flexible wire generously coated with rubber that you can wrap around the rod, leaving the twists

Cable ties repurposed as on-line rod storage. Their flexibility makes them easy to mount on your rod. MORGAN LYLE

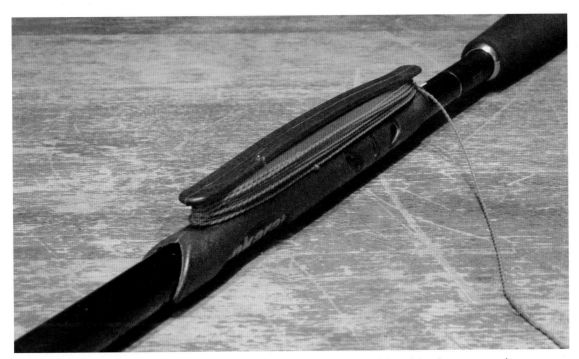

The Snap-On Line Winder has the advantage of easily attaching to and detaching from your rod. MORGAN LYLE

sticking up. You can wrap your line around these twists just like with the EZ Keepers. (I soon realized these are nothing more than household cable organizers from the hardware store, so I bought mine at Home Depot and felt proud of paying a couple bucks less. I do like them.)

Another storage device I like is the Snap-On Line Winder. I bought mine from Dragontail Tenkara, whose main product is a nice line of moderately priced rods. It's essentially a narrow spool about 6 inches long, with a foam core you can stick your fly in to keep it secure. In case the rod you use is thinner than the part that snaps over the rod, there are foam shims to fill up the space so the keeper stays on snugly. I like this one, too.

CHAPTER 14

Rigging Up Your Tenkara Rod

Setting up a tenkara rod for fishing is considerably simpler than rigging up a fly rod. Basically, you attach the line, extend the rod, and you're ready to go. Once you're used to handling the gear, it can take less than a minute, and that's part of the satisfying simplicity of tenkara fishing.

Tenkara rods vary in their length, weight, stiffness, and action, and there is even more variety in the kinds of lines you can use. But the basic setup is always the same. You attach a line to the tip of the rod, and attach a tippet—a few feet of fine, clear fishing line—to the other end of the line. You tie a fly to the end of the tippet.

Here's the procedure in more detail.

Connecting the Line to the Rod

There are two ways to attach the line to the lillian, that short strip of (usually) red braided nylon at the very tip of the rod. The first method is to use a Girth Hitch Knot. This is how you will attach a line with a loop at its rod end, a feature usually found on floating or braided lines. The second method, considered the traditional Japanese way to attach a level line, is to tie a simple Arbor Knot in the line, run the lillian twice through the knot's loop and tighten. The Arbor Knot is easy to make—just tie an overhand knot around the line, with a Figure 8 Knot tied at the end of the line as a stopper.

You'll start with your rod in its collapsed state and your line wound onto a line-holder spool. You can attach the line with most of it still wound onto the spool,

Tom Sadler about to attach his line to his rod. A few simple knots and connections put the tenkara rig together. MORGAN LYLE but I usually unspool the whole line first and let it lie on the water or on the ground at my feet, and stash the spool back in my pack.

If you're using a line that attaches with a Girth Hitch, reach through its loop with your thumb and forefinger, grab the line and pull it back through the loop, forming the new, double-stranded loop that will slip over the lillian. If you use an Arbor knot and don't have one already tied, you'll need to tie it now. Either way, the idea is to have the connecting method you use ready to go at this point.

Turn your attention now to the rod. Remove the tip plug and put it in a safe pocket where you won't lose it. You now need to get your rod's lillian exposed, so you can connect the line. You want *only* the lillian exposed; keep the rod sections, especially that fragile tip section, safely collapsed together inside the handle section. Just tip the rod upside down while using a finger or two to prevent all the sections from slipping out. You'll intuitively figure out how to shake the lillian out.

Now, if you're Girth Hitching, slip the loop you made over the lillian, fold the lillian down and hold it there (so there's no chance of yanking the fragile rod tip sideways), pull the line tight and snug it up against the overhand knot near the lillian's tip. If you're using an Arbor Knot, slip the lillian through the knot's loop *twice*, fold it down and hold it, and pull the line tight. You don't need to snug this up against a knot in the lillian.

Important: *Make sure you're only pulling against the lillian, and not exerting any sideways pressure on the tip section of the rod.* Accidentally pushing or yanking the rod tip sideways is by far the most common cause of tenkara-rod breakage. I've done it myself a few times.

All that's left now is to extend the rod. That's pretty straightforward. Do not swing the rod like a toy lightsaber. Rather, pull the sections out one by one, snugging the butt of each one lightly into the tip of the next. Don't snug them too hard, just tight enough that the smaller section doesn't slide back into the larger.

Disconnecting the Line

A key difference between tenkara and fly fishing is that while a fly rod will generally stay set up until the outing is over, you're likely to unrig and rerig the tenkara outfit at least a couple of times during the day. Taking the line off the rod is surprisingly easy—so much so that the first time you do it, you may wonder how the line stays connected in the first place.

Why remove the line? You may decide a different line is called for; maybe when evening falls, the thin level line you used in the afternoon becomes hard to see and you want something brighter or thicker. Maybe you're fishing a smooth, flat pool and want to drift a dry fly down to a rising trout using a floating line, as in regular fly fishing. Perhaps you're finished with a smooth pool and are about to fish faster water with lots of pockets and seams, where a level line will let you drop the fly with precision. Maybe a breeze has come up that makes a heavier braided line easier to cast than a feather-light level line.

Or maybe you want to move to another spot, and getting from here to there involves a walk through woods or over rough terrain, where carrying a fully extended 12-foot rod with a fragile tip is asking for trouble. In this case, collapse the rod, wind the line onto a spool, and drop the spool over the rod shaft, or wind the line onto an on-the-rod line holder. Now you have a rod less than two feet long that's easy to carry anywhere.

Adding Tippet to the Line

Theoretically, a tippet is a more or less invisible connection between the casting line and the fly. Casting lines aren't invisible at all; a fly line is a small PVC-coated cord, and even though a tenkara level line is much smaller and lighter than a fly line, it's still readily visible to the fish. Tenkara braided and floating lines fall somewhere in between a level line and a fly line.

When you're fishing, you want to keep any of these kinds of line away from the fish. The sight of a casting line on or above the water can spook them. So you use a tippet—a segment of what most people think of as fishing line: fine, clear monofilament. Is it actually invisible to fish? Almost definitely not, but it seems to be unobtrusive enough that they don't mind its presence.

Fly fishers have a leader at the end of their casting lines, consisting of tapered clear monofilament, with a few feet of tippet at the end of that. The tenkara rig is simpler: just some tippet, usually 2 to 6 feet, tied to the end of the casting line.

There's more discussion of what kind and size of tippet to use in the chapter on lines. Let's talk now about how to connect a tippet to a casting line.

Again, it depends on the kind of line you're using. Tapered braided lines usually have a loop at the end, and that allows for my favorite way of connecting any two segments of fishing line, the loop-to-loop connection. Make a loop in the end of the piece of tippet you're tying on using a Perfection Loop, Non-Slip Loop Knot, or my favorite, the simple Surgeon's Loop. Pass the loop at the end of the casting line through the loop in the tippet, then pass the fly end of the tippet through the loop in the end of the casting line and pull the tippet through. The two loops will "shake hands" with each other, and it's impossible for them to come apart. Best of all, you can reverse this attachment method to remove the tippet without damaging the line.

Some tenkara lines come with a small, metal tippet ring. You could do a loop-to-loop attachment with a tippet ring, but most people just tie the tippet to the ring with the same kind of knot they would use to tie the tippet to the fly. I'm not crazy about tippet rings, but they're very easy to use.

Things are different with level lines. For one thing, they don't come with any loop or ring, because you make the lines yourself by cutting off the appropriate length of line from a spool. So you build your own attachment device. You can tie on a tippet ring (they're sold commercially) with the kind of knot you would use to tie on a fly (more on that in a moment). You could make a small loop in the end of your level line, using any of the knots mentioned above.

Or you could use the method popular with many Japanese tenkara anglers: tie a Figure 8 Knot in the end of your line to serve as a stopper, then tie your tippet to the line just above the stopper, using the same knot you would use to tie on a fly. Slide that knot down to the stopper.

If these knots are new to you, it might be a good idea to practice them at home rather than trying them for the first time on the water. In fact, you can attach your tippet to your tenkara line at home, saving yourself the time and trouble when you fish. If it turns out you need a longer tippet, it's easy enough to tie on some more with a Surgeon's Knot or, less easily, with a Blood Knot. If for some reason you need a shorter tippet, just snip some off.

Tying on a Fly

You can attach the fly to the tippet with any knot you prefer. I and many others, fly fishers as well as tenkara folks, have become fond of a quick, simple knot called the Davy Knot. It was invented by a man named Davy Wotton, a native of the U.K. who now lives near the great Ozark Mountains trout rivers of Arkansas. Davy has been a fly-fishing entrepreneur all his life. His knot is easy to tie and just as strong as any other.

Line is attached to rod, tippet attached to line, fly tied to tippet—you're ready to fish. Breaking down the rod, when you're done for the day or taking a break or moving to another spot, consists of reversing the steps. In almost every case you can leave the fly on the tippet if you want, since tenkara fly-line holders are designed to accommodate them. And unlike fly reels, tenkara lines are wound onto their spools fly-end first.

Knots and Connections

Simple as a tenkara rig may be, you still need to use a few knots and connect the components. These are the ones I use. There are others, and you may find others you like better, but these work fine for me.

A couple of thoughts on knots. It really is helpful to practice them at home before attempting them on the water with the clock ticking and trout rising. It is also helpful, unless you have

sharp, young eyes, to have some kind of magnification handy—Flip-Focals are awesome, but drugstore reading glasses will do. Being able to see what you're doing, especially when working with the fine lines used in most fishing for trout and other modest-sized freshwater fish, is essential.

Line-to-Rod Knots

Floating, tapered nylon and furled lines all come with a little loop of string at the rod end. This loop is used to make Girth Hitch, also called a Lark's Head or a Cow Hitch. This very simple connection creates a new loop in the end of the line; you slip that loop over the lillian, pull it tight, and snug it up against the lillian's overhand knot.

To release the line from the lillian, pull on the lillian and the tag of the knot in the string loop on the end of the line. The Girth Hitch will come loose immediately.

A different knot is used to attach a level line. These do not have a loop of string at the rod end; you make an Arbor Knot, a simple slip knot, in the monofilament line itself and tighten it onto the lillian. The Arbor Knot is nothing more than an overhand knot tied around the line. That forms a loop. You slip that loop over the lillian and pull the tag of the knot to tighten.

Pass the lillian through the loop of the Arbor Knot twice for a more secure connection.

When taking the line off the rod, all you have to do is pull the lillian and the tag of the Arbor Knot. The slip knot will loosen and can be pulled free of the lillian.

With either the Girth Hitch or the Arbor Knot, make sure the rod tip is fully inside the

ATTACHING A FURLED OR TAPERED LINE
TO A ROD USING A GIRTH HITCH

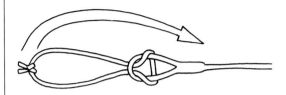

1. Bring the loop back toward the standing line.

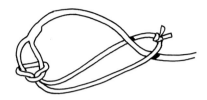

2. Pull the standing line through the loop, which creates another loop.

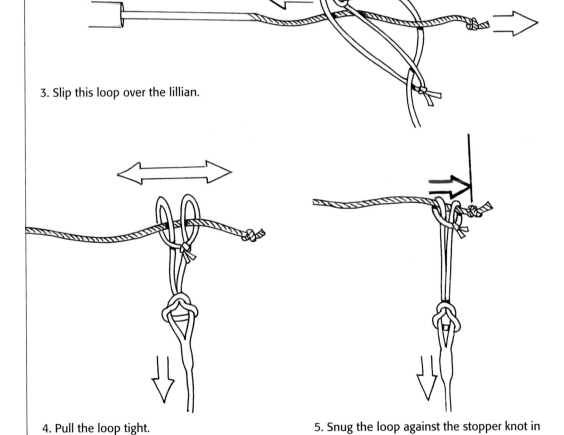

3. Slip this loop over the lillian.

4. Pull the loop tight.

5. Snug the loop against the stopper knot in the lillian.

ATTACHING A LEVEL LINE TO A ROD
USING AN ARBOR KNOT

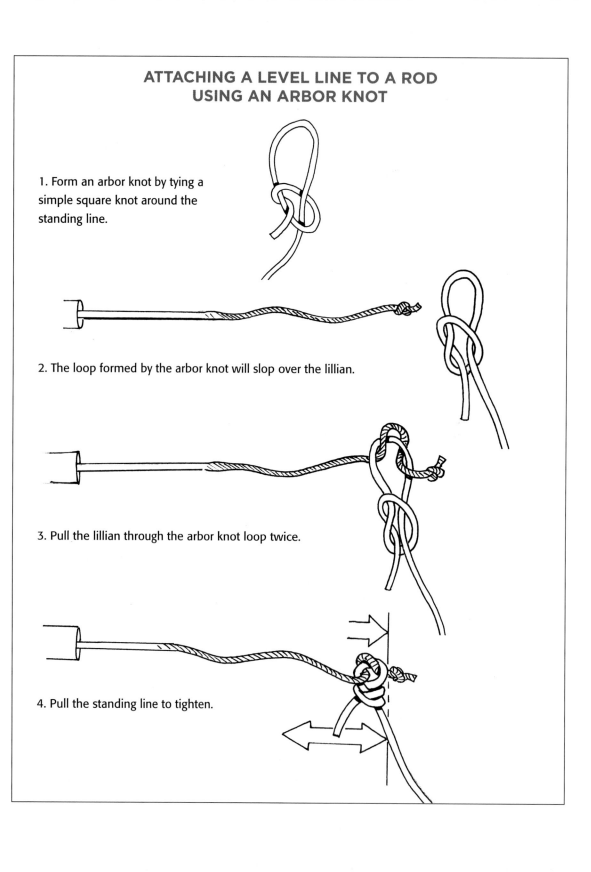

1. Form an arbor knot by tying a simple square knot around the standing line.

2. The loop formed by the arbor knot will slop over the lillian.

3. Pull the lillian through the arbor knot loop twice.

4. Pull the standing line to tighten.

other sections of the collapsed rod; if the tip is extended, it's too easy to concentrate on the knot and not realize you're bending the tip sideways, which can easily cause it to break.

Tippet-to-Line Knot

Most furled lines have either a loop or a tippet ring at the end. If it's a loop, you can attach your tippet with the loop-to-loop connection, described below. If it's a tippet ring, you can tie on the tippet the same way you would tie tippet to a fly. But if you're using level line, you'll have to make other arrangements.

The classic Japanese technique is to make a stopper knot in the end of the line, then tie your tippet onto the line, using the same knot you would use to tie your tippet to the hook, and snug it up against the stopper knot. I don't care for this method. I prefer to make

loops in the end of the line and the tippet, and put them together using a loop-to-loop connection.

The easiest knot for making a loop is the Double Surgeon's Loop. You fold the line back along itself, then tie an overhand knot in it. The "double" part is simple, passing through the fold of the line back through the loop of the knot a second time.

An objection you hear to the Double (or Single) Surgeon's Knot is that the loop is slightly canted. Other knots, such as the Perfection Loop, avoid this cant. But I've never found it to be a big issue, in fly fishing or tenkara.

The loop-to-loop connection is a simple and foolproof way to connect two lines with looped ends. Pass the loop in the end of the line through the loop in the tippet (I say "big through the little" to remind myself which goes through which). Then take the free end of the

LOOP-TO-LOOP CONNECTING IS A FOOLPROOF WAY TO JOIN TO SEGMENTS OF LINE, OR CONNECT A LINE TO A TIPPET.

1. Slip the loop at the end of the standing line through the loop in the line to be attached. Then pull the end of the line to be attached through the loop in the standing line.

2. With the two loops in a "handshake," pull both ways to tighten.

tippet and pass it through the loop in the end of the line. Pull them tight, and the two loops will form a "handshake" connection.

Many tapered (and untapered) nylon lines have blank ends where the tippet attaches. In the case of tapered lines, you can just make a Double Surgeon's Loop and use the loop-to-loop connection. Untapered lines are a bit thick at their tips for the Double Surgeon's Knot. Your options here are to make a stopper knot and tie your tippet to the line, as mentioned above, or to attach a short piece of sturdy mono-filament and attach your tippet to that, with the Double Surgeon's Loop / loop-to-loop connection or simply tying the tippet on with a Double Surgeon's Knot.

How do you attach the short piece of mono-filament? The best knot for this kind of thing is the Nail Knot, discussed below.

Adding Tippet

From time to time, you'll need to make your tippet longer. Maybe your tippet will break when fighting a fish, or maybe you'll get your fly caught on something and have to pull on the line and break it off. Maybe you'll decide you need a couple more feet of tippet to reach the spot you want to fish. Or you may decide to add some finer tippet to approach a cautious fish or tie on a very small fly.

Again, there are more complex knots that have stood the test of time, but I prefer the very simple Double Surgeon's Knot. It's basically the same procedure as the Double Surgeon's Loop. Lie the ends of the two pieces you want to attach next to each other and tie a double overhand knot in them together. Pull tight and trim the tags. There are a number of excellent online resources for this knot. You can also use a stan-dard Blood Knot.

A Loop-to-Loop Connection from Line to Rod

I have experimented a bit with attaching a loop to the lillian of my rod, and using that to attach the line with a loop-to-loop connection. The Abor Knot and Girth Hitch work fine, but I used the loop-to-loop connection for so long in fly fishing before I started tenkara fishing that I've become a fan of its common-sense design and sturdy structure.

There are, however, two obvious drawbacks. One is that the entire line must be free, so that it can be pulled through the loop attached to the lillian. This means you must remove the line from its spool first. That's not a huge deal when your whole line and tippet are only around 16 feet long, but it will feel like an interruption of your work flow if you're accustomed to attach-ing the line first, then unspooling it.

The other drawback is that attaching a loop to a lillian requires a knot that's fussier than any of the others described here, the Nail Knot. The good news is that you only have to make it once and can do it in the comfort of home.

You could make the loop connector out of heavy monofilament, perhaps a short length of level line. I use fly-line backing, which is simply a fine, strong string. Attach it to the lillian with the Nail Knot then make a loop in the end with a Double Surgeon's Knot. The length of this loop connector doesn't seem to matter, but I like to keep it to three inches or so.

Your floating/tapered/braided line already has the loop necessary for the connection. To

A loop-to-loop connector for fly line to rod, made of fly-line backing nail-knotted onto the lillian.

SUSAN EPSTEIN

THE DAVY KNOT IS QUICK, EASY, AND STRONG.

1. Run the tippet through the eye of the hook.

2. Tie an overhand knot.

3. Run the tag of the overhand knot back through the loop.

4. Hold the tag and the standing line and pull tight.

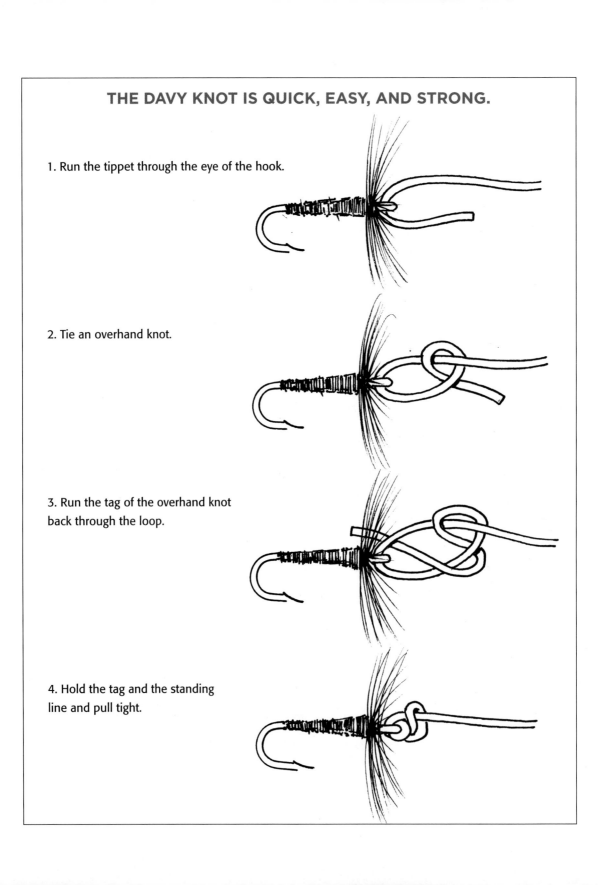

attach a level line, make a Double Surgeon's Loop in the rod end of the line and make a loop-to-loop connection, big (loop connector) through little (loop in the line).

Tying the Fly to the Tippet

There are many knots for tying line to a hook. Probably the best known and most widely used is the Clinch Knot. But for some time now, I have been using the Davy Knot. It's simpler, quicker, stronger, and wastes less line. It's basically just a simple overhand knot, except you pull the tag end of the line back up through the loop. Pull the tag and the line to tighten the knot.

CHAPTER 15

Fixed-Line Fishing for Species Other Than Trout

I n Central Park in New York City, a few minutes' walk from Strawberry Fields, stands one of the world's most famous fountains, on the shore of Central Park Lake.

The central sculpture of Bethesda Fountain is twenty-six-feet tall and its pool is almost a hundred feet wide. The pool sits in the center of two-level Bethesda Terrace, built during the Civil War, with grand staircases connecting the upper terrace to the lower, which extends to the shore of the lake.

On Sunday afternoons in nice weather the plaza is thronged with tourists and native New Yorkers alike. On one particular Sunday afternoon Dennis Kim and I put on a show for them, pulling hefty carp out of the lake, using what amounted to a really big tenkara rod.

I lost count of how many people asked us in an hour's time whether we were in fact allowed to fish there, and what kind of fish we hoped to catch. Each time the 21-foot Nissin Kiyogi carp rod bent double and we pulled the big brown fish to Dennis's net, the onlookers whipped out their phones for pictures and video. Most assumed the lake held nothing more than the red-ear slider turtles that regularly poked their heads above the water for a breath.

"It's almost like a performance," said Dennis, a twenty-nine-year-old college-admissions consultant, who traveled from his apartment in the Bronx with his collapsed rod in a four-foot case and his big folding net in a long, zippered bag.

Dennis Kim with a Central Park carp, caught with bait on a 21-foot, fixed-line Japanese rod. MORGAN LYLE

"You're talking to someone and you have to do a hook-set. It can look a little uncivilized."

A New Jersey native, Dennis is a cheerful guy and generous with his time when passersby ask about his fishing. They often inquired about the bait, and he would insist they take a sniff of his little Tupperware container of canned corn marinated in strawberry banana Jell-O. When a tough guy sitting nearby gruffly warned us he wouldn't wait for the cops if we hit him with a hook, Dennis—in slacks and shiny oxfords from an appointment earlier in the day—told him, "Don't worry about it." And when one of the dozens of rowboats plying the lake on the chilly late-April day blundered into our target water along the plaza, he was more forgiving than a lot of fly fishers I know would have been.

"Unfortunately, you get that a lot," he said. "It comes with the territory."

The boat didn't slow the fishing. Dennis used what's known as a hair rig, a device invented in Europe, where carp fishing is a really big deal. The hair rig has a small loop of fine cord extending from the eye of the hook; Dennis used a needle with a handle and a hooked point to impale a stack of four of the plumpest corn kernels in the container, then hooked the end of the cord loop and slid the kernels down onto it. His line was rigged with a narrow ten-inch float of varnished balsa wood with neon red and yellow on the upper end.

You don't want to make a backcast on a crowded plaza, so he pointed the long rod at the water, pulled back on the line with his other hand to flex the rod, then let the rig fly. It's known as a bow-and-arrow cast and was popularized by renowned trout angler Joe Humphreys, who teaches fly fishing at Penn State

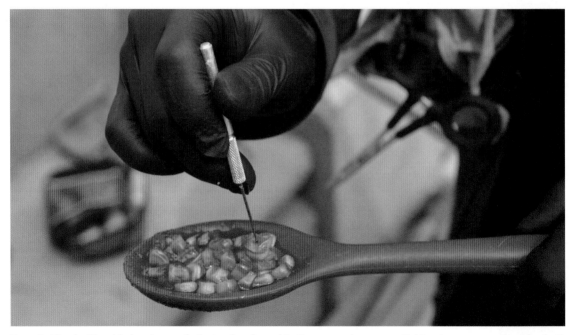

Dennis Kim baiting his hook on a hair rig, developed in Europe, where carp fishing is very popular. The bait is corn marinated in strawberry Jell-O. MORGAN LYLE

Those New York City carp will put a bend in your rod. Dennis Kim plays another large fish at Bethesda Fountain. MORGAN LYLE

University. Dennis's float and bait shot to the full extent of the line, right where he wanted it. The corn settled to the bottom and he held the rod and waited.

Four times, we didn't have to wait long. The float would sometimes quiver when a turtle was nibbling at the bait, but Dennis knew better than to set the hook. When a carp grabs the bait and turns to leave, the float just disappears.

"We need full commitment," Dennis said. "It has to unreservedly go down."

This is obviously not tenkara fishing; tenkara is by definition fly-fishing for trout, and we were bait fishing for carp. But it was fixed-line fishing, and very similar to tenkara except for its scale: the direct connection to the fish, transmitting every movement of the wild animal on the end

of the line; the big flex of the rod, absorbing the carp's lunges and runs. The similarity that struck me most was the efficiency: Each of these carp was in Dennis's net in under two minutes. Carp that big caught on a fly rod and reel would have been allowed to run all over the lake, laboring to get away, dragged back in, running again, for heaven knows how long, by an angler marveling at how strong the fish is.

Actually, the last fish took a little longer than two minutes, because I broke Dennis's rod.

Dennis had kindly handed the Kiyogi off to me after casting the bait. In a few minutes, the float unreservedly went down, I set the hook, and the fish was on. I thought I did a good job playing it, but as I horsed the carp toward the bulkhead of the plaza, I had the rod nearly directly upright—skittish about lowering it to the side on account of all the nearby civilians—and that's one thing you shouldn't do with a big fish on a fixed-line rod. The second section from the top snapped.

The snap of a rod is a small but sickening sound, especially if it's someone else's rod, and most especially if it belongs to someone you

Jeff Dannaldson of Overland Park, Kansas, with one of the nice bass he catches on tenkara rods on a regular basis. JEFF DANNALDSON

barely know. But we managed to land the fish, and buying a replacement section from Ten-karaBum.com was easy, so all ended well.

Dennis is a tenkara fisherman, too. Like many New Yorkers, he doesn't own a car, but he's been known to take the Metro-North commuter railroad to stops north of New York City, where small streams connecting the city's upstate drinking reservoirs provide optimal trout habitat and good trout fishing. (The Bethesda Fountain, in fact, was erected to commemorate the opening of the first aqueduct to bring clean upstate water to crowded, un-sewered, choleric Manhattan.)

Dennis has also used the big Kiyogi (with flies, not bait) on the Delaware River, holy trout water to a generation of eastern fly fishers. But when he's not trout fishing, he's fixed-line fishing for the big carp of Central Park.

"From Day One," many tenkara anglers say, American fly fishers used the fixed-line rods originally designed for trout fishing to catch species other than trout. After all, not everyone lives near a glittering trout stream.

"It's at least a two-and-a-half-hour drive to the nearest trout fishing," said Jeff Dannaldson of Overland Park, Kansas.

Jeff's been a fishing nut as long as he can remember, since his boyhood summers at the family camp on Lake of the Ozarks. When he discovered tenkara rods, he fell in love with their no-nonsense casting and the stealth they made possible. He fishes the heavily stocked spring creek trout parks of Missouri and likes it well enough, and the big dam-fed rivers of Arkansas, with their jumbo trout, are a reasonable destination.

But true mountain trout streams don't exist in the Midwest. So Jeff's "bread and butter" fishing

If they're within range, you can catch striped bass (and almost any other kind of fish) on fixed-line rods. Chris Stewart with a Massachusetts stripah. CHRIS STEWART

Gamefish such as bluefish and striped bass often come close to Atlantic coast in search of prey. It's easy to toss a streamer fly into their hunting grounds with a tenkara-rod designated for bigger fish. JESSICA LYLE

is for bass, channel catfish, crappie, and bluegill on a variety of tenkara and *keiryu* rods, mostly Japanese imports, in the lakes, ponds, and rivers near home. "I've got a city park lake that's just a couple of blocks from my house," he said. "I can walk to it."

Tenkara and *keiryu* rods are designed for trout, but you can use them to fish for any freshwater fish species within casting distance. For that matter, you can use fixed-line rods for saltwater fish, as Tenkara Bum Chris Stewart has demonstrated on the striped bass flats of Cape Cod, using a Kiyogi carp rod like the one I broke. There are large, trout-less swaths of the US where lots of

people do lots of fishing, and some of them like doing it with tenkara-style rods.

"There seems to be two camps of tenkara: 'Do it exactly the way they do it in Japan,' and 'I wonder what I can do with this?'" Dannaldson said. "I'm in the latter camp."

I think a lot of fixed-line anglers spend time in both camps. Here in New York State, there's tons of great trout fishing, and I've caught trout on tenkara gear in most of the celebrated streams. But I, too, have a city park lake I can walk to; there are no trout in it, but there are panfish and largemouth bass. The mighty carp of Bethesda Fountain are only a subway ride

away, and carp are abundant in ponds a short drive from my home in the outer boroughs and on Long Island.

Carp on Flies

It has been kind of surprising to see the homely common carp earn the admiration of the American fly-fishing community. Until relatively recently, these anglers disdained the "coarse" fish near their homes and traveled to the

A Utah carp poses with ERiK Ostrander of Tenkara Guides LLC. The guides were among the first people to attempt catching carp on flies with tenkara rods in the United States. ERIK OSTRANDER

The Tenkara Guides love trout in mountain streams as much as anyone, but they also make time to try for heavy carp in brown water under highway overpasses. ERiK Ostrander shows one off. ERIK OSTRANDER

mountainous regions to catch trout, which were pretty and tasted good. I once saw a grouchy old fly fisherman catch a bass while trout fishing and throw it up on the bank to die, flapping and suffocating. Why? "It's a bass," he scowled.

Carp were held in even lower regard. Said the late fishing writer and editor John Merwin, acknowledging that a growing number of fly fishers considered carp smart and fun to catch, "Yeah, but they're still carp." (Merwin did also say he expected fly-fishing for carp to become a big deal and, as usual, he was right.)

A younger generation of fly fishers has rejected the fish bigotry of their forebears and embraced the *Cyprinus carpio*. The obvious attractions are that carp are abundant and big. Practically everyone in the country has a body of water nearby with carp in it; unlike trout, they can tolerate water that is murky, dirty, and warm.

The original American fly anglers loved the taste of trout and dragged pack-baskets full of them down from their trout camps in the mountains. The catch-and-release ethos prevails in modern times. Carp fishing is catch-and-release, too—not so much as a matter of conservation, but because carp aren't considered a food fish for most Americans. So, between the fact that hardly anyone wants to eat them and the fact that they can live in almost any river, lake, or pond, carp are all over the place. From their

Karin Miller with a big tenkara-caught Colorado carp. Her company, Zen Tenkara, specializes in rods designed to handle large fish. KARIN MILLER

The upper Rondout Creek in New York is a pristine trout stream, but near its confluence with the Hudson River, it's a great place to catch bass on flies. MORGAN LYLE

native ranges home in Europe and Asia, they have been introduced to, and thrived on, every continent except Antarctica.

If you get a kick out of catching big fish, you'll love carp. Even small ones are heavy and strong. Fish of five to ten pounds are very common, and a fish that size is a hoot on any fly rod, fixed line or reeled. Carp are not, however, acrobatic like trout and salmon. They fight doggedly, but not urgently. Mostly, they try to swim away, and the challenge for the angler is to turn them and pull them back.

While their size is fun and their availability is convenient, the thing that fly fishers seem to like best about carp is that they're not pushovers.

They are quite willing to take bait—all fish are—but to get them to grab a fly requires a fair amount of luck and skill. They have keen senses of sight and smell and are considered smart fish.

Carp primarily eat what they find on the bottom of the river or pond, and that includes plants as well as organisms like worms, aquatic insects, and crustaceans. Some dedicated carp fly fishers consider it important to use flies that resemble the local forage; others stay with general patterns that have been proven to catch carp and other species in the past. If you're fishing for carp in a public park, where people throw little cubes of white bread to ducks or geese, you may want to use a fly that looks like a little square of Wonder Bread. I'm serious. I know a guy who does it.

Even if you manage to figure out the perfect fly to use, you still have to convince a carp to eat it. It's very common to see carp swimming within casting range that simply cannot be caught. They are not feeding. You'll see them cruising, often in small groups, or even rolling and thrashing at the surface. Sometimes they just seem to be lounging around. It's understood among carp fishers that casting to these fish is a waste of time. They're not hungry.

Fortunately, it's easy to tell when carp are actively feeding: You'll see little plumes of mud rising from the bottom where they have been rooting around with their snouts. Find a carp doing this, drop a fly close enough to be seen but not close enough to be startling, give the fly a small twitch or two, and you have a good chance of catching a strong fish. This kind of fishing is sometimes compared to fishing for bonefish in the Florida Keys. The strategy and the technique are quite similar. The difference is instead of wading a sandy flat in the topics, you're on the shore of a muddy pond in upstate New York or wherever.

Provided you can reach the fish, I think fixed-line gear is well suited to fishing for carp. You can use a light level line and hold it entirely off the water, slipping your fly in front of the fish with utmost stealth. A stout tenkara rod should be able to control a modest carp well enough, and it's even possible to land the big ones, provided you use sideways pressure to turn the fish.

At this writing, I know of two sources for true fixed-line carp rods made by Asian companies: TenkaraBum.com and AllFishingBuy.com, both in New York City. But several American tenkara-rod companies sell rods specifically designed for large fish, which are fine for carp fishing.

Tenkara for Bass

In all likelihood, the first non-trout fish caught on a tenkara rod in the US was a bass. Largemouth and smallmouth bass are the most popular gamefish in the United States, and as with carp, they're much more widely available than trout. They are willing, and sometimes eager, to bite a fly, and they're really strong. The original expert on fly-fishing for bass, Dr. James Henshall, wrote in 1881, "I consider him, inch for inch and pound for pound, the gamest fish that swims."

"They might be the most fun of all on tenkara rods," Jeff Dannaldson said.

Bass will often bite trout flies, though many anglers use them in larger sizes for bass than they do for trout. Flies designed specifically for bass, like floating foam poppers that draw dramatic strikes at the surface, can be used with a tenkara rod.

Flies in the streamer category, which are designed to imitate little fish, work well for the aggressive bass, although I've always felt at a bit of a disadvantage when using them with fixed-line rods. When you're fly-fishing, you can make a long cast and then pull the line back through the guides, making the streamer fly swim as you retrieve it. You can't retrieve line that's tied to the tip of your rod, so to make the fly move, you have to use the whole rod to pull it through the water. It works well enough, but the length of the swim is quite limited. So it's important to get the fly into the most likely bass-holding water.

In my first summer of tenkara fishing, I caught a bass while trout fishing on the upper end of the East Branch of the Delaware River. I knew it was a bass because I had caught a glimpse of it during the fight, but even if I hadn't seen it, I might have guessed from its behavior. While I have caught bass that leapt like salmon, most often they fight from the deepest water they can reach, pulling with impressive strength. This one fought hard, then parked at the bottom of four feet of water, close to where I stood.

This wasn't a great big bass, but there was no budging it. Eventually I lost my patience, and learned my first lesson in hand-lining fish: Wait until the fish is ready. Holding the rod behind me, I was able to reach the line, which was stretched as tight as the high E string on a guitar. At the moment I touched the line, the bass made a lunge and the line snapped. Had I waited, it would probably have gotten tired of the tug-of-war, and I may have been able to bring it to hand. Bass are strong. Act accordingly when landing them.

I've caught lots of bass, most as bycatch when I was looking for trout, but sometimes by choice. One upstate New York river I like to fish looks like a trout stream, with lots of places to wade, but the water is too warm for trout. It's fine for bass, so that's what I catch there, along with red-breasted sunfish that punch way above their weight.

Tenkara-Perfect Warm-Water Fish

The United States would be a great market for tenkara rods even if there weren't a single trout in the country. Fish like bluegill, sunfish, pumpkinseed, and crappie are found coast to coast, and they are roughly comparable in size and strength to the Japanese trout for which tenkara gear evolved. They're scrappy and pretty, and some are considered delicious.

Somewhat larger fish like pickerel and modest pike will challenge a tenkara rod. Large pike and muskellunge, which have surged in popularity among fly fishers in recent years, can be hooked and landed with rods designed for large fish from American companies like the Zen Tenkara Zaka or the Badger Tenkara Wisco 2.

But it's the panfish that are perfect for classic tenkara. Pike and even bass are usually fished for with flies that are kind of a pain to cast with tenkara rods due to their size—at least two or three inches long. It can be done, but it's a little ungainly. Bluegill and crappie, on the other hand, are used to diets of small insects and other organisms, just like the little half-inch flies tenkara rods cast so beautifully. They will bite the same dry flies and wet flies and nymphs we cast for trout, as well as small versions of the floating poppers that are so much fun when fishing for bass.

They can be greedy little buggers, too, attempting to eat flies that are too big for them. The many red-breasted sunfish I caught while fishing for bass on that upstate New York river ate a pretty big fly, a beefy inch-long (size 8) nymph pattern known as a Girdle Bug, black with wiggly white rubber legs. Most of the time I thought I had caught a bass until I got the sunnies close enough to see what they were.

Jeff Dannaldson used to live right next to a private-park lake in the St. Louis metro area that had "absolutely monster bluegill." The wide, flat body of a panfish presses against the water like a canoe paddle and provides a

Bluegills are a blast on tenkara gear. MORGAN LYLE

surprisingly strong fight that bends a tenkara rod deeply. But like most fish, a crappie or glue-gill will pretty quickly sense the futility of fight-ing that big, soft spring, and once the initial panicky struggle is over, can be brought to hand in a more or less orderly manner.

Chances are there are bluegill or crappie or sunfish in a pond or slow-moving river near you. You can fish for them with any tenkara rod. A light rod will be more pleasant to cast, and the fight with the fish will be more exciting. A stan-dard 12-foot trout rod will be fine. Naturally, if you're fishing a large body of water, a longer rod will extend your range.

You can also use any line you like—fluorocar-bon level line, tapered braided line, floating tenkara fly line, with four feet or so of 5X tip-pet. Since this kind of fishing is usually done in lakes, ponds, or rivers with very slow current, you'll need to give your fly a little action. You can experiment to see what kind of movement provokes a response from the fish: quick and erratic, slow and rhythmic, or even just letting the fly sink for those fish who like to strike "on the drop," as they say.

A few wet flies, a few nymphs, and maybe a cou-ple of small streamers should be all you need. It's easy enough to poke around online and see if there are any patterns favored in your area, or simply any fly that strikes you as a good bet. Panfish are opportunistic eaters, accustomed to a wide-ranging diet, and not fussy about flies.

A net isn't absolutely necessary since panfish are of modest size, but having one will make it easier to scoop them up and prevent them from being injured while you land them.

Trout often share their streams with fallfish or chubs, which are not generally thought of as "game" fish—although after having hooked them I have often thought of them as game-fish until the end of the fight when the fish got close enough to identify and I realized they weren't trout.

CHAPTER 16

Euro Nymphing: Tenkara's European Cousin

Tenkara bears a striking resemblance to one of the most popular trends in mainstream fly fishing: Euro nymphing. The method was developed by European competition fly fishers to maximize the number of fish they catch while complying with the rules of the Fédération Internationale de la Pêche Sportive Mouche or, in English, the International Sport Flyfishing Federation, usually referred to as FIPS Mouche.

The key elements are long rods, short lines held high off the water, and simple flies that suggest aquatic insects in a general way.

National teams in Poland, France, Spain, the Czech Republic, and other European countries have competed for decades on a circuit that culminates in a World Championship, compete with an Olympics-style opening procession and medal stand. American fly fishers joined the circuit in a serious way in the mid-2000s.

In the United States, local and regional competitions serve as qualifiers for a National Championship, which picks the team that will go to the World tourney.

The very idea of competitive fly fishing is mildly controversial among anglers. Some see it as a corruption of a contemplative pursuit. But for those who enjoy it, especially younger anglers, competing adds a new level of interest to the fishing.

At least in the United States, competition anglers receive no pay or subsidy, except perhaps a small sponsorship here or there. They fish on their own time and pay their own way, often driving hundreds of miles to competitions and

Pat Weiss of Pennsylvania, one of the country's top competition fly fishers. European-style competition angling has much in common with tenkara. MORGAN LYLE staying in motels. The traveling and socializing with their fellow competitors is all part of the fun, but it's also a significant effort and expense. So you can be sure these guys and gals are going to use the techniques that are most likely to catch fish.

I've hung around a couple of local competitions as an observing journalist. They're fun. US competitors have set up various kinds of competitions, and even established a team-based league that sanctions events, mainly in the eastern part of the country.

Despite the fact that anglers compete as individuals and members of teams, they fish individually, much as they would purely for their own fun. The difference is there's another person standing by with a clipboard, recording their catches, making sure they follow the rules, and letting them know when their time slot, usually three hours, is up.

They fish on public water, and they don't have it to themselves—recreational anglers can and do fish alongside them. For that matter, the water is liable to be used by kayakers or tubers, too, which adds a layer of challenge to the fishing. Each angler is assigned to a "beat," usually a couple hundred yards of stream, and every fish caught above a certain size is recorded for their score.

Many comps, especially the larger regional ones, also have beats on lakes, which are fished from shore or even from boats. But it's always trout fishing, and it's mostly stream fishing.

Within that category, the anglers sometimes use floating dry flies to catch fish feeding at the surface, and that kind of fishing usually involves picking a fly that looks as much as possible like the real ones. Comp fishers also sometimes fish with streamers, sunken flies that look like small fish, or other calorie-rich critters like crayfish or leeches, made to "swim" well below the surface.

But more than anything else, competition fishers endeavor to catch trout with nymph flies, which are meant to look like the underwater life stage of mayflies, caddisflies, or stoneflies.

Flies that Win Trophies

Lots of fly fishers use nymphs, and for the same reason the comp anglers do—they are very effective fish catchers. Nymphs are fished deep in the stream, down in the depths where trout hang out most of the time. They are meant to drift along with the current, making them easy for trout to grab as a quick snack.

The European comp anglers began devising nymph patterns with particular characteristics. Instead of being fitted with "hackle" feather fibers meant to simulate legs or tails, the Euro nymphs are sleek, usually just a body, often tapered, and made in such a way to look segmented, like many insects.

The nymphs are designed this way to help them sink readily. The more quickly they get down to the depth where the fish are holding, the better the chance of catching a fish. The Euro nymphers decided this tactical advantage was more important than any attempt at imitating specific insects.

Often the Euro nymphs have a metal bead at the front of the fly. Bead-head flies existed before comp anglers began using them, but they became important to the competitors for a couple of reasons. One is that the metal bead adds to the fly's sink rate. In recent times, many anglers have switched from beads made of tin to

One of New York comp angler Loren Williams's fly boxes, with an array of salmon egg, worm, and nymph patterns. MORGAN LYLE

ones made of tungsten, which are considerably heavier. FIPS Mouche rules forbid using sinkers attached to the line, so any sink weight needs to be built into the fly itself.

The other advantage of a bead-head fly is that the bead adds a little flash. It increases the fly's visibility and catches the trout's attention.

Euro nymphers also borrowed a page from the bait-fisher's book by using jig hooks for many patterns. Flies tied on these hooks ride with the hook point up instead of down, which reduces the possibility of snagging on rocks and branches lying on the bottom of the stream, and usually results in a secure upper-jaw hookup.

Heavy Flies, Long Rods, and Short Lines

When the situation calls for fishing a floating fly, comp fishers often employ the standard fly-fishing setup, with a thin clear leader 9 to 12 feet long at the end of a floating fly line. But for their nymph fishing, they developed a radically different rig.

A very common recreational-fishing method of fishing nymphs is to use a strike indicator, which is basically a little bobber, usually made of foam, from which the nymph is suspended on a length of leader about equal to the depth of the water being fished. The angler watches the indicator float and sets the hook when it is pulled underwater by a fish that has grabbed the nymph.

Again, FIPS Mouche rules require a work-around; strike indicators are not permitted in competitions. So Euro nymphers, especially French and Spanish anglers, essentially jettisoned the traditional fly line-and-leader arrangement.

They adopted rods as long as 11 feet, compared to the traditional 9-foot fly-rod length.

They also began using very long leaders. In fact, they often fished only with their leaders. Comp anglers still had floating fly lines on their reels, but often the line never even made it into the cast. The leaders could be around 20 feet long, and the anglers used them to fish water as close as right under the rod tip and seldom farther than twenty feet away from where they stood.

Euro nymphers make quick, flicking casts, dropping the nymph into every pocket that could conceivably hold a fish. The rod is high and the line is tight, with little or no slack. Tournament fly fishers did not invent tight-line nymphing, also known as high-stick nymphing, but they elevated it to an art.

Comp anglers "fish with their feet." They run their nymphs through each likely spot two or three times, and if there is no bite, move onto the next spot. Each pocket of "soft," current-free water behind a midstream rock, or the "seam" between a swift current and a slower current alongside, would be checked for fish. Sometimes the angler sees his or her line dart, or quiver, or pause, indicating a fish has taken the fly. Sometimes they feel a tug before they see anything. Any interruption of the progress of the line downstream during the drift prompts the angler to set the hook.

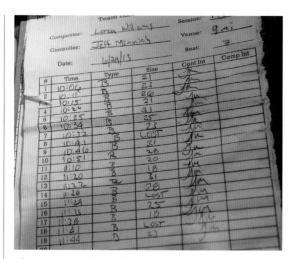

Nineteen trout in under two hours for Loren Williams, in a tournament on Nine Mile Creek in New York. MORGAN LYLE

This is very similar to tenkara fishing, with one key difference. Authentic Japanese tenkara fishing uses unweighted wet flies, which have similarly simple construction but do have a hackle of feather fibers at the front of the fly, and fishes them shallow, usually just a few inches below the surface. Nymphs are designed to be fished deep.

It is true that some Japanese tenkara fishers like to use weighted nymphs, for the same reason as their peers in Europe and America, both competitors and recreational anglers.

American anglers quickly recognized how effective tenkara rods could be for presenting nymphs. I sure did. The first time I caught a trout with a tenkara rod, the fly I was using was a heavy, olive green Euro-style grub pattern. I have caught hundreds of trout nymphing with a tenkara rod since then.

The willowy action of a tenkara rod poses a bit of a problem when using a weighted nymph.

The rod's flexibility makes it a little more difficult to set the hook of a fly drifting three or four feet deep. Some tenkara rod models, however, have somewhat stiffer actions, specifically to make them more suitable for nymphing, both casting and hook setting. The manufacturer will usually make that clear.

Open Loop and Water Hauling

Having a weighted nymph on the end of a tenkara line is a little clunky to handle. When using a virtually weightless wet fly, a tenkara rod provides a silky smooth casting stroke. Casting a heavy nymph on the end of a tenkara line—or a fly-line leader, for that matter—feels more like throwing an Argentine bola. It's hard to be as precise about where your fly lands. And I suppose it's technically not true fly fishing, since you're not casting the line but rather flinging the weighted lure itself. (Again, this is true with a fly rod, too.)

Fly fishers know to "open the loop" on their cast when tossing a heavy fly. The loop is the

Casting heavy flies, like this Euro-style nymph by Anthony Naples at Three Rivers Tenkara, requires a slower casting stroke. MORGAN LYLE

long U-shape the line makes when it has been flung into a back or forward cast. A narrow "U" results in quick line speed, which helps your line stretch out to its fullest extension—in other words, maximum casting distance—and it also affords the best control of where your line and fly are headed.

Getting that tight loop is a goal of good casting in both tenkara and fly fishing. It's easy to master with an unweighted fly. But a weighted nymph has its own momentum. Snapping the kind of authoritative cast that generates a tight loop is not a good idea with a tungsten-weighted fishhook.

To open your loop, make your movements slower and gentler. The "U" shape will look more like a "C." This reduces the chance that the nymph will bang into the back of your head, or strike the rod on its way to the water, which creates little stress fractures that can result in rod breakage when fighting a fish.

The Water Haul

In many cases, you won't need to make a loop in your line at all. A simple, highly efficient technique known as the water haul eliminates the need for a backcast.

The name "water haul" means the water itself loads, or flexes, the rod, so it can spring into the forward cast and fling the line where it needs to go. Here's how it works. Your fly will have finished its drift and be hanging downstream of you. Your rod will be pointing at the fly, or at least be pointing downstream. You just give the rod a little tug in the upstream direction, then come to a stop, just like making a forward cast. The line will carry the fly back up to the general area where your drift began and you can

I've never fished in a tournament, but when nymphing with a rod and reel, I try to do what the comp guys do. The techniques of tenkara and Euro nymphing are remarkably similar. SUSAN EPSTEIN

conduct another drift, in case there's a trout in the area that didn't notice your fly the first time.

The key is to smoothly accelerate your rod as you lift the fly from its dangling downstream position. By going slowly at first, you allow the water to hang onto your fly long enough to bend the rod. Once you have some flex in the rod, it's easy to make a cast that travels perpendicular to you, downstream to upstream.

The water haul is the most efficient kind of fly cast. It wastes no time, and there's no risk of getting snagged on trees or brush during a backcast. With a little practice, you'll be doing it without thinking about it.

An interesting note about picking up your fly at the end of the drift to make another cast: It's surprising how many trout you catch at this very moment. It may just be dumb luck, with a trout having noticed your fly just in time to

grab it. In some cases, it may be that the trout has followed the fly as it drifted downstream, and sees the sudden rise of the fly to the surface as its last chance. It may be that the drifting fly was of no interest, but a fly that darts to the surface, as yours will when you're lifting the rod for another cast, rings the dinner bell.

There's not much you can do to prepare for it, beyond being aware that it might happen. When a trout does take a fly in this situation, it usually hooks itself. It's fun, expecting to make a routine cast and suddenly feeling the weight of a fish.

Leading the Fly

As your nymph drops into the water and drifts downstream with the current, you won't see it, but you'll see your line angling down into the water. The point where the line pierces the surface will move downstream at the speed of the current. You'll want to "follow" it by moving your hand across your body in the same direction as the current, which allows the drift to continue until you run out of reach and the fly starts to swing across the stream below you.

The classic Euro nymphing technique is to "lead" the fly, by having the rod tip a little downstream of the fly's position. It's almost as though you are pulling the fly downstream. This keeps you tightly connected with the nymph, ready to set the hook at the slightest indication that the drift has been interrupted, hopefully by a trout having taken your fly.

In some cases, it actually is good to pull the fly downstream a little faster than the current. If a dead drift isn't working, it's worth a try; sometimes fish are willing to attack a fly that seems to be racing downstream faster than the current. Leading your flies can also prevent them from dropping all the way to the bottom, which can save you a lot of grief when the streambed is snaggy with rocks and woody debris.

Whether you are leading the flies or simply letting them drift with the current, there will be no slack in your line, and that's a huge advantage. You'll be aware of anything affecting the fly's natural drift, and you'll be able to react to it with a small, quick motion—so quick you often won't even be aware you've done it until after you've caught the fish.

Fishing at the Right Depth

The general idea of nymph fishing is that your fly should drift along just above the streambed. If your fly isn't getting stuck on rocks or logs, it is said, you're not fishing deep enough.

Using a strike indicator to suspend your nymph and split-shot sinkers on the line to pull the fly down to the bottom is an effective way to fish. Some say it's the most effective method of all. Your fly is near the fish, and the indicator lets you know when a fish has grabbed the fly and it's time to set the hook.

But, as noted, this kind of rig isn't allowed in many fishing tournaments, so Euro nymphers learned to fish without them. The sighter on the line took the place of the foam strike indicator, and the heavy flies made sinkers unnecessary. But one function of the indicator-and-split-shot setup remained to be addressed: keeping the fly at the right depth.

When the nymph is suspended from an indicator, you can move the indicator up or down the leader to change the depth at which the nymph drifts. When there's nothing but a straight line/leader between your rod and your fly, you adjust the depth simply by raising or lowering the rod tip.

That's pretty foolproof. Your one concern when tenkara fishing would be to keep the end of your brightly colored casting line above the surface, so that only the leader is underwater. Even this is a guideline, not a firm rule. If you have reason to think there might be a trout at the bottom of a five-foot pool, and you only have 4 feet of tippet, you could take the trouble to lengthen the tippet, or you could take your chances and let 1 foot of casting line hang below the surface.

It should be pointed out that you are completely free to use split-shot and strike indicators in your tenkara fishing. I know of one guy in particular who prefers to do so, and he catches lots of fish. Still, learning to sink your fly, control its depth, and detect strikes without having to fuss with bobbers and sinkers is a liberating experience.

CHAPTER 17

A Tenkara Angler's Gear

A key aspect of the tenkara ethos is to keep gear to a minimum. Some of us are better at it than others.

Tenkara is, after all, a form of fly fishing, and fly fishing is a gear-heavy game. The Japanese founders of the sport prided themselves on carrying only a small fly box with a few simple flies and a few necessary gadgets, and many American tenkara anglers honor this tradition.

I must confess I'm not there yet. I may never be there. I was a fly fisher for twenty-five years before I discovered tenkara, and a key aspect of the fly-fishing ethos is to carry lots of flies so you'll be prepared for any situation.

I do think there's some truth to the contention that Japanese tenkara anglers can get away with using fewer kinds of flies because their fishing is more narrowly defined. Generally, a Japanese tenkara angler will fish small- to moderate-sized mountain streams for trout. Simple size 12 flies generally suggest aquatic insects well enough to catch trout in this kind of environment.

But when I grab my sling back and go fishing, I might be headed to a larger river with deeper pools, or a cold, slow river with profuse hatches of specific insects, or even to a river or pond that holds bass or carp instead of trout. All those situations call for flies other than Japanese-style *kebari*. The big, deep pools might need flies with heavy beads to help them sink quickly. It might be necessary to use flies that "match" that profuse hatch. And I may want to use streamers or popping surface bugs for the bass.

Adam Klagsbrun carried all the gear he needed for an evening of fishing on Boulder Creek in this little pouch. A line, some tippet, a few flies, and a couple of simple tools are all that is required. MORGAN LYLE

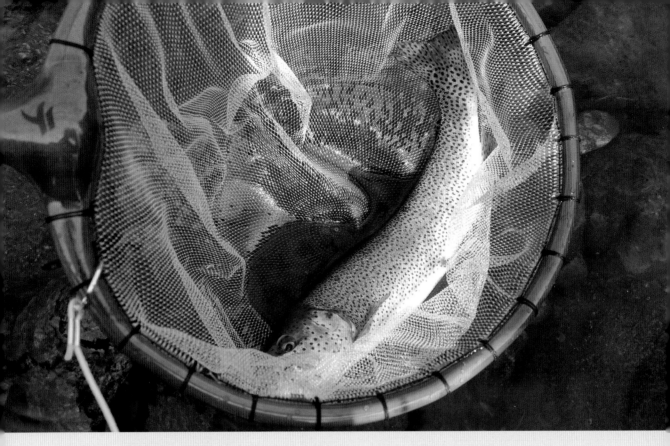

THE *TAMO*, A TENKARA-STYLE NET

There is no good reason to go fishing without a net.

Well, maybe if you're halfheartedly fishing for bluegills in a pond where they're abundant and you're really not worried if some get away, you don't need a net. But if you want to make sure you land the fish you hook, you should use one. What's more, a net can make the process of being caught much easier on the fish, and even prevent them from being injured. A wriggling fish can be difficult to control and it's not uncommon for them to bang into rocks in the shallow water at your feet as they struggle to escape. Scooped up in a net, they're safe.

Japanese tenkara anglers use a style of net called a *tamo*. It is both elegant and functional in design.

A *tamo* has two distinctive characteristics: It has a round hoop, whereas most Western landing nets are oblong or teardrop shaped; and its handle angles away from the hoop.

The small opening put me off at first. For several years now, I've been carrying a large net of the style favored by many competition anglers, a Frabill model with a long dimension of 21 inches. It's almost comically large for trout fishing, but comp anglers want to land every fish they catch, and so do I.

The *tamo*-style landing net is effective for catching trout and easy to carry in your belt. MORGAN LYLE

The round opening of a typical *tamo* net, on the other hand, is 10 to 12 inches wide. That's fine for smaller trout, but I worried that it wouldn't be big enough for a big trout—and big trout are the ones I'm most concerned about landing.

But as Chris Stewart at Tenkara Bum has pointed out, trout bend. As it turns out, I've had occasion to land trout up to 16 inches or so with a *tamo* with no trouble at all.

The angle of the handle makes the *tamo* easy to carry in your wading belt. It causes the hoop to lean away from your back for comfort.

It is entirely possible to carry a standard Western landing net with the handle stuck through your belt and the hoop pointing up, but the weight, shape, and size of most nets argue against it. Most Western anglers hang their nets from a loop just below their necks on the back of their fishing vests or packs.

I've found that I really like carrying the little *tamo* in my belt. And now that I've begun using a sling pack instead of a vest or a satchel, hanging a net isn't an option. The whole point of a sling pack is that you sling it around to the front when you need to retrieve something, then sling it back to the rear to get it out of your way. You can't be slinging a pack around with a landing net attached to it.

Tamos have even become a do-it-yourself item for some tenkara anglers. Here's the idea: You keep an eye out for a pine tree branch about an inch thick, with two smaller branches sticking out from it at 90-degree angles, perfectly opposite each other. When you find such a thing, you cut the branch at the length you want your net's handle to be, and cut the smaller perpendicular branches so they're long enough to curve around to meet each other with a little overlap, forming a loop of the appropriate size. The wood is allowed to dry for a month, the bark is peeled off, the small branches are bound and glued, the whole thing is smoothed down and prettied up, and a commercially available net bag is attached.

It's a cool project that I may undertake one day. For now, I'm perfectly satisfied with a store-bought *tamo*. Tenkara USA sells a nice one, and models by Shimano and Daiwa can be found at TenkaraBum.com and elsewhere. They all come with a lead you can clip to any handy loop to make sure your *tamo* doesn't float away if it slips out of your hand or your belt.

Eliminating unnecessary gear is part of the tenkara ethos. Some of us are better at it than others.

SUSAN EPSTEIN

It must be noted that *kebari* can be used in all these situations, sometimes very effectively. But often, there will be better choices. And for me, that means multiple fly boxes.

And yet, I must also confess it is highly likely that most of the flies in the five boxes I carry will not get wet once over the course of an entire season. What can I say? It comforts me to have

them on hand. Besides, part of the fun of fly fishing, for me anyway, is experimenting with what kind of flies fish will take. I like having the option of doing that.

I'm even worse with lines. At present, there are twelve lines or spools of level line in one pocket of my sling. That doesn't count four spools of tippet (3X, 4X, 5X, and 6X). I could almost certainly get through any day of fishing with a fraction of that stuff. A couple of lines were purchased several seasons ago, and are still in their unopened packaging. I tell myself I'll experiment with how different lines perform on different rods, since that is also part of the fun, but then I fish the same line on the same rod all day.

Guys like Adam Klagsbrun carry just a small pouch, with a small box of flies, maybe a spare line and a spool or two of tippet. That's the austere end of the spectrum. I suspect the correct amount of stuff to have lies between Adam's bag and mine, but closer to his. There are any number of fishing vests, chest packs, waist packs, satchels, and sling packs on the market. In terms of purely fishing tools, I think you could get away with a gear load something like this, and find the right-sized pack to carry it in, in whatever style you prefer. (Do as I say, not as I do.)

One 3x4-inch, six-compartment box with twelve dry flies: whatever style you prefer, six dark colored and six light colored, with two of each color in size 18, two in size 14, and two in size 12. Even better, three in size 16 and three in size 12.

(A substantial segment of the fly-fishing world finds it necessary to make, carry, and use flies as small as size 24. I don't. If I found myself on a flat pool with an extraordinary number of extraordinary fish rising to flies that tiny, I might consider it. But that scenario is mostly absent from my life, and frankly I don't miss it.)

Another six-compartment box with an assortment of *kebari*, in sizes 14, 12, and 10, perhaps with a couple as big as size 6.

A small slit-foam nymph box, again with a dozen flies (yes, it's a tradition to carry even numbers of things, and dozens or half dozens are especially popular). Nothing smaller than 18 is necessary. Some should have tungsten heads for when you need to fish deep. Killer Bugs, Gold-Ribbed Hare's Ears, Princes, and Pheasant Tails will meet your needs, but there are a gazillion great nymph patterns and you should carry the ones you like.

Finally, a few modest, lightweight streamers, perhaps a couple of Woolly Buggers and Gartside Soft-Hackle Streamers, both in size 10, for those times when your big fish would rather eat a little fish than a bug.

You do need more than flies, however. A nipper to snip off bits of tippet after tying on a fly or lengthening a leader is pretty necessary (your dentist will agree), and keeping it on a retractable zinger will make your life easier. A pair of hemostats makes it much, much easier to remove a hook from a fish's mouth, both for you and for the fish. A small magnifier that clips to the brim of your hat or a pair of reading

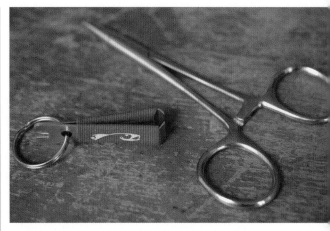

Two on-stream essentials: a nipper for clipping off flies or excess line from knots, and a hemostat for removing hooks quickly and humanely from the fish's mouth. MORGAN LYLE

glasses will help anglers of a certain age, especially with small flies or fading light.

A headlamp or small flashlight is a very good idea. Insect repellent and sunscreen are essentials. If you're going to be more than a few footsteps from your car for any length of time (and I hope you are), you should have some water and a snack with you, and probably a small, basic first-aid kit.

If you're a fly fisher, you already know about this stuff. If you're new to the game, you'll probably find there are other must-haves as you go along, depending on your personal tastes.

The American Tenkara Industry

Soon after she launched Zen Tenkara in 2012, Karin Miller learned in no uncertain terms how threatening tenkara seemed to some in the fly-fishing business.

"I got physically pushed out of a fly shop," she recalled. "I went in trying to talk to them about tenkara and show them my rods, and literally was told it was people like me who would be the death of fly fishing. There was physical contact."

That's probably an extreme example, but there is no question tenkara got a lukewarm welcome at best from the fly-fishing establishment. While she was a bit shocked at getting the bum's rush from that shop in Colorado, Miller said she understands the circumstances in which it happened.

"A lot of fly-shop owners were really angry," she said. "They didn't want to hear that you needed one fly that was really easy to tie and a $150 rod, because they're thinking, how can I make money on this?"

In the early days, I wondered whether the American fly-fishing scene would absorb tenkara—whether the time would come when I would flip through the latest catalog from the Sage or Winston fly-rod companies and come to their lines of tenkara rods. It never happened. Except for Temple Fork Outfitters selling one rod bearing its label, and Orvis carrying a Tenkara USA model the same way it carries Swarovski binoculars, none of the big fly brands have joined the tenkara market.

"We had the discussion" about making Orvis tenkara rods, said marketing director Tom Rosenbauer. But making telescoping rods would require a whole new

---

Yes, that's a shark. Zen Tenkara founder Karin Miller's version of tenkara goes way beyond trout in mountain streams. KARIN MILLER research-and-development project and a whole new manufacturing process. The company was already selling regular fly rods as quickly as it could make them. "The CEO is working in the rod shop on weekends," Rosenbauer said.

There was one other reason not to start selling Orvis tenkara rods, he said: "Did we want to do that to Daniel?" Galhardo and Orvis had a relationship that worked for them both. There was no need for Orvis to crush Tenkara USA with the competition. So a mom-and-pop tenkara-rod industry grew up in the United States, alongside the fly-fishing industry.

It was inevitable that American entrepreneurs would decide to launch their own tenkara companies. Despite Rosenbauer's reservations about having to retool to get into the tenkara business, starting one's own tenkara company wasn't all that hard. Factories in China and other Asian countries had been making tenkara rods for decades. You could order a batch on Alibaba.com, have your logo applied just above the handle, put up a website, and presto, you're a tenkara company.

There was disdain in some corners for off-the-shelf tenkara rods, especially as American anglers learned more about the sport and "real" Japanese rods became available in the US (mainly through TenkaraBum.com).

There were also reports of tenkara-rod designs being stolen by manufacturers and sold to other would-be tenkara brands. Tenkara USA sued a fly shop in Colorado for selling a rod it claimed was made to the same specs, in the same factory, as one of TUSA's popular models.

They may not have quite the exquisite feel or fit and finish of rods produced by Japanese companies, but the mostly Chinese rods sold by Tenkara USA, Tenkara Rod Co., Zen Tenkara,

Badger Tenkara, Tenkara Tanuki, Three Rivers Tenkara, Dragontail Tenkara, Fountainhead, et al., are perfectly serviceable, enjoyable to use and own, and have caught many fish.

For that matter, there are some fine products made in Chinese factories. Chris Stewart at Tenkara Bum—American tenkara's leading authority on Japanese rods—has, for example, called the Chinese-made Daiwa Expert LT H44 "the world's best 'big fish' tenkara rod." Of course, as Chris points out, the rod was designed by a Japanese company with long experience in making tenkara rods.

The American rod companies maintain that they, too, have designed their rods and tested prototypes to be sure their customers will enjoy them.

Different Country, Different Fishing

Miller "got into fly fishing because I was a Miami girl who's been transplanted to Colorado and needed water, and I found myself attracted to the waters here." She enjoyed fly fishing up to a point, but didn't feel drawn to a lifetime of study of the lore, the equipment, the techniques. "When I tried a tenkara rod for the very first time, it was like, why the hell haven't I been doing this from the beginning?" she said. "This is great. This is awesome. More people need to know about this. I felt like I was at the beginning of something, and if I was feeling that way, a lot of other people were feeling that way."

"And being in Colorado, most of the time, a reel is not necessary," she said, referring to the state's many trout-filled small streams.

When she launched her own tenkara company, Karin didn't feel welcome in the young tenkara market and decided to appeal to regular fly fishers. Japanese tenkara fishing might involve light tackle for small trout, but she would offer her American customers strong rods for big fish.

"I've spent the last several years making rods I think regular fly guys would like," she said. "In the fly-fishing world, what is badass? Carp. Salmon. Shark. Permit. Bonefish. Steelhead. Golden dorado. That's where you earn respect."

So she sells rods designed to handle that kind of fishing, roughly the same length as trout rods but stronger. She travels to big-fish destinations like Alaska and the Caribbean and South America and has her adventures filmed for promotional videos.

Miller got married in 2018 to a lawyer named Todd Fischer—who had represented Tenkara USA in its trademark infringement against the fly shop in Denver. It was pure coincidence, she said, "but, yeah, he had heard of tenkara when we started dating."

Zen Tenkara's challenge to its customers is to rely on technique to catch and land big fish the truly old-fashioned way, without the assistance of a reel.

"When you have a reel you've got a tool, a mechanism, that's doing it for you," she said. "You take that away, it's you, the rod, and the fish."

Karin has gotten some guff for her exploits with salmon and shark on beefed-up tenkara rods. But the impulse to try to catch large fish with a fixed-line rod isn't limited to westerners.

In the early years of American tenkara, many of us, stung by tenkara being dismissed as a tiny-fish game, cheered a video of a man named Choji Hosoyama catching steelhead trout with a fixed-line rod in British Columbia.

Steelhead fishing is one of those macho categories. These migratory trout grow really big

Karin Miller giving a talk on tenkara. "More people need to know about this," she said. KARIN MILLER

and really strong in the Pacific Ocean (and the Great Lakes). Many times over the years, tenkara skeptics have said something like, "Let's see you land a steelhead with one of those things." Hosoyama did just that. He wasn't tenkara fishing; he used bait, not flies, and his rod was twice as long, and much stronger, than a tenkara rod. But it worked the same way. He had no reel, no reserve of line that would allow a strong fish to speed away. He fought the salmon with nothing more than the flex of his rod and his own ability to move. He did have a guide with him who netted the fish at the end of the fight.

Hosoyama, like Karin and many American anglers, wanted to experience the challenge of landing big fish on a fixed-line rod. It's not such a crazy idea.

Badger Tenkara cofounder Matt Sment. JAMES GILL PHOTOGRAPHY

Matt Sment and Mike Lutes don't think it's crazy. Friends since kindergarten in Rockford, Illinois, who parted ways after high school but ended up both living in Madison, Wisconsin, years later, the two men launched Badger Tenkara in 2014.

"I had not fly-fished before I picked up a tenkara rod," Sment said. "I was a very casual bait-and-bobber angler." But he was an outdoorsman, and was putting together an ultralight backpacking kit when Lutes brought tenkara to his attention. "He said, 'Hey this kind of complements what you're doing, you should check it out.'"

Sment tried out a rod from Tenkara USA, and while he caught no fish that first time, he was nonetheless "instantly enchanted."

Sment joined the army in 2005, and after his hitch, worked as a contractor for the military at various posts around the country, training soldiers, homeland-security personnel, and police. But a decade later, he was in a time of transition.

Something about tenkara's purposefulness and precision, its "tactical aspect," appealed to his background in the service and his love of nature.

"I decided I wanted to focus on something positive and outdoors, and put my energy into a passion," he said. So he and his boyhood fishing pal started a company, "because we wanted to increase opportunities for people to experience tenkara fishing."

Sment and Lutes undertook the study of tenkara as a method of trout fishing, "but also to push the limits in fishing for bass and pike and musky and all these other fish," Sment said. "We've combined that attitude and that sense of exploration with what we consider a reasonable price point."

Badger's most expensive rod was $115, about half of what most of their competitors charged. Even so, the company's rods have been well received, by customers who range from retirees returning to fishing after a long absence to young people and "people who were anglers as a secondary activity, backpackers or paddlers or what have you."

Badger was an early proponent of fly-fishing-style floating lines and "took a lot of guff for that off the bat," but it was comfortable for experienced fly fishers and for newbies, because the weight of a floating line makes it easy to feel and control while casting.

Unlike the long-established fly-fishing industry, every tenkara company has to teach prospective customers not just how to use the gear, but also why. Badger, Sment said, made sure to explain that a tenkara rod is not just a reel-less version of a fly rod but a fishing tool of its own, to be used in particular ways in order to take advantage of its characteristics. "Check out what we can do with a 12-foot rod that has the right flex profile," he said.

In April 2019, Sment announced that Badger was leaving the retail rod business, though not closing up. "The company's going to be focused on content production," he said. "I'm going on an indefinite road trip to fish and interview and film and get around North America, and explore what tenkara in America is. He said the change was driven by personal as well as professional reasons, but acknowledged the tenkara rod market is "already well-served."

"Between the American companies and Japanese companies and Amazon, it's kind of a challenging space," he said. "It pretty much already has everything it can hold."

Making Rods in the USA

Miller, meanwhile, embarked in 2018 on an ambitious project. She set out to make Zen Tenkara the first company to manufacture tenkara rods in the United States.

The top models of the top brands in the regular fly-fishing market (all models at some of them) are made in the US. Many fly fishers are convinced that the American-made models are superior to imports from China or Korea, and many like the idea of supporting American companies and workers. There are also scores of rods made in Asia that sell for about half the price of the American-made rods. They fish just fine, and many fly fishers can't afford to spend upwards of $1,000 on fishing rods, so they fill a need. Those willing to invest in American-made rods do so out of pride of ownership and appreciation for top-level craftsmanship.

At this writing, virtually all tenkara rods in the United States are made in Asia. Those manufactured in Japan by Nissin, Suntech, Daiwa, Shimano, or Tenryu are seen the same way that Americans see American-made fly rods, in terms of design, build, and fit and finish. Some of those companies also outsource the manufacturing of their rods to China, Vietnam, and Thailand, and those rods are held in similarly high regard because of their brands' reputations.

All the American tenkara companies, including Zen, send their designs to Asian factories

Karin with an Alaskan arctic char. In 2018, Zen Tenkara was working to become the first company to manufacture tenkara rods in the US. KARIN MILLER

for manufacture, and all have loyal fans in the American tenkara community. Fisher said there's a market for American-made rods.

"For one thing, I like the idea of something made in the United States," Miller said. "I will have more control over my designs, and making changes and modifications and testing rods and developing rods and all of those things are simplified. It's so hard when you're dealing with overseas manufacturers, and it takes so long, and you have no control over what happens with your design and your specs."

"Conversations don't have to happen at three o'clock in the morning" she added, with a laugh, referring to the time difference between Colorado and China. "And I love the idea. My reputation is what other people have called a fusion of tenkara and Western fly fishing, and the way we are using the tenkara rod as a tool, I think we're not traditional. Our philosophy is very American, and I think it fits us to offer a rod made in the United States, rolled on mandrels that were made in the United States."

Daniel Galhardo expressed interest in manufacturing in the US as far back as 2012, and told me six years later he is still considering the idea, or at least setting up a workshop to develop prototypes or make limited runs of specialty rods.

However, he also said manufacturing in China adds to, rather than takes from, employment in the United States.

"I strongly believe we are part of a global economy, and if it were not for the factories in China, which I started working with at the beginning, tenkara would not have been introduced here," he said. "It sometimes upsets me how people do not see the value of an interconnected global economy and sometimes think producing overseas takes jobs away," he said.

"Yes, we work with China to make our rods, but without their support there would be at least thirteen to sixteen fewer jobs in the US from my company alone (six direct hires and up to ten indirect, such as the line makers we hire, fulfillment center employees, business support staff, packaging people, etc). That's not to count the other people employed by other tenkara companies directly and indirectly at this point, or the staff or sales support at retailers that carry our brands."

Lost in Translation

Tenkara arrived in the US with an origin story. Japanese mountain men of centuries past fished for trout in rugged mountain country with a simple fly, a horsehair line, and a rod made of a bamboo stalk. It wasn't a hobby, it was a job—the *shokuryoshi* were commercial fishermen who sold their catch to restaurants, hotels, and shops.

It became a hobby in the mid-twentieth century, when a small segment of the recreational fishing community availed itself of modern tenkara rods, made of fiberglass or carbon fiber, and took to the mountain streams to fish for small trout in idyllic surroundings.

The United States has idyllic mountain streams, too, and tenkara worked just as well here as it did in Japan. But Americans did not limit themselves to mountain streams. They used their tenkara rods on larger rivers to catch larger trout, or in slower, warmer rivers to catch bass, or in lakes and ponds to catch whatever may live there.

Nor did they limit themselves to using a simple fly consisting of a feather and thread wrapped onto a hook. With their new tenkara rods, Americans used the same flies they fished with their fly rods. Some were designed only to float, some were weighted so they would sink straight to the bottom, some were designed to be towed through the water to look like a small swimming fish.

Daniel Galhardo at Tenkara USA never demanded that his customers use their tenkara rods to catch only small trout in small streams. He did, however, take every opportunity to teach Americans about the exquisite pleasure of Japanese-style

Go Ishii fishing in Japan. Tenkara evolved on the streams of the Japanese mountains, but tenkara rods are used in many environments, for many species, in the West. GO ISHII tenkara. But it was largely to no avail. Americans wanted to buy his rods and use them to fish for all kinds of fish, in all kinds of waters.

Almost as soon as it arrived in the US, tenkara became something different than it had been back in Japan.

Throwing Rods into the Water

The founder of the outdoor gear company Patagonia, Yvon Chouinard, had been one of Daniel Galhardo's heroes. Chouinard's book, *Let My People Go Surfing: The Education of a Reluctant Businessman*, was a big influence on Galhardo's own business aspirations. Chouinard was a role model for Daniel, not only in his approach to commerce but also in his love for the outdoors:

mountain climbing, surfing, and, it turned out, tenkara fishing.

Chouinard and Hisao Ishigaki were the big names at Tenkara USA's first tenkara summit in West Yellowstone, Montana, in August, 2011. But Chouinard would soon go from friend to competitor. By 2012, he was consulting with Temple Fork Outfitters (TFO), a Texas-based fly-rod company, on the company's plan to start selling its own branded tenkara rod.

TFO was the first and only major fly-fishing company to sell tenkara rods under its own label. It was a big moment for the tenkara movement. Patagonia, meanwhile, published a book by Chouinard, fly-fishing celebrity Craig Mathews of Montana, and Italian fly fisher Mauro Mazzo, titled *Simple Fly Fishing: Techniques for Tenkara and Rod & Reel*. Patagonia bundled

Daniel Galhardo, Hisao Ishigaki, Yvon Chouinard, and Craig Mathews at the first Tenkara USA summit in 2011. MORGAN LYLE

the book with TFO's tenkara rod and sold it online and in its tony stores. Tenkara USA suddenly had some formidable competition.

Simple Fly Fishing, however, strayed pretty far from the Japanese method of tenkara fishing. Most notably, Chouinard and Mathews advocated a technique that struck some tenkara anglers as bizarre: when attempting to subdue a large fish, throwing the whole rod into the water and waiting until the fish calmed down, then wading in, retrieving the rod, and landing the fish.

"The rod will swing downstream of the fish and tire it out," Mathews wrote. "It may take a while, but good things come to those who wait." Later, Chouinard recalls throwing his tenkara rod three times while fishing for salmon one week in Iceland. "I ran as fast as I could in the waist-deep water but could never catch up to my waking rod handle," he wrote. "But after seventy-five yards, I saw my rod turn and come back upstream. I ran back up and caught up with it near where the fish took the fly."

The idea of chasing big fish with rods meant for small ones had a real-life impact in New Hampshire. Fly fishers there demanded, successfully, that tenkara be kept out of some of their best streams.

New Hampshire had set aside some sections of some rivers as fly-fishing-only waters. These designations usually come about when local anglers fear that fishing with bait or lures will injure too many fish. Trout often swallow baited hooks, and the treble hooks of spinning lures can be devilish when trying to release fish. Fly fishing is generally considered less injurious than other methods.

Tenkara is certainly fly fishing. But New Hampshire's fishing regulations define fly fishing as using a rod with a reel. Tenkara anglers asked the state to change the regulations so tenkara would be legal on the fly-fishing-only streams, but fly fishers voiced their opposition.

"No one thought beaching or throwing the rod in after a 2-pound rainbow or a 20-inch landlocked salmon would be the best for the fish," recalled David Poole, who was president of the New Hampshire Guides' Association at the time. "Even the act of playing the fish until one could land it 'hand over hand' [another suggested technique] would be detrimental for the fish."

Frankly, I think most tenkara rods are capable of landing those fish unharmed.

But I don't blame the New Hampshire guides for not wanting to see their best trout dragging rods behind them, or flopping on the rocks because the angler used more line than he could manage.

Tenkara, Americanized

Tenkara USA made it quite clear from the start that tenkara consisted of fishing for modest trout in mountain streams. So did the new enthusiasts who had launched tenkara websites and blogs. But we couldn't help ourselves. We had to find more ways to play with our new toys.

"They did it, they enjoyed it, and they became more interested in what else is there," recalled Brian Trow from Mossy Creek Fly Fishing in Virginia. "It became, 'I've got a rod, a line, what's next?' What I liked watching, and being a part of, was trying to adjust and adapt it to all the waters in this country, and all the species and all the different bugs and all that stuff.

"Catching bigger fish than most people think you can on tenkara, casting bigger flies like

Adam Klagsbrun is a champion of authentic Japanese-style tenkara fishing, for trout in mountain streams. You can fish for bass, carp or other species with fixed-line rods, he maintains, but you shouldn't call it tenkara. MORGAN LYLE

mouse patterns, and being able to set the hook and playing the fish in, and putting some of those notions that this is a tiny, fragile toy down. We had fun doing that, letting people realize that 'here it is, this is what you can do with these things, these are really strong fishing tools.' It was all fun.

"We were going to tinker with it. We were going to push the limit."

American retailers like Trow and Matt Sment of Badger Tenkara tend to emphasize the challenges and advantages of the fixed-line nature of tenkara rods rather than their suitability for

mountain streams and trout. The direct connection of line to rod, the stealthy stalking at close range, the ability of the long, flexible rod to subdue fish—those are the key elements, no matter what species is on the end of the line.

"Badger Tenkara was almost called Access Tenkara, and that's been our core goal, to get tenkara rods into people's hands and to get them out on the water experiencing them," said Sment, Badger's cofounder. "Not being overly picky in supporting a vision of that, and being supportive of whatever vision the customer chooses. Not only to learn Japanese tenkara styles and study Japanese masters, but also to push the limits in fishing for bass and pike and musky and all these other fish."

Even Chris Stewart of Tenkara Bum, who may have done more than anyone to teach Japanese tenkara to the Western audience, has always encouraged his customers to use the premium Japanese rods he imports for whatever species they like, in whatever waters they like. Stewart is dismayed by what have been called the "tenkara wars," windy online arguments about what is and isn't real tenkara. At one point, he posted a tagline on TenkaraBum.com that said, "Bastardizing tenkara since 2010." In 2017, he added another: "I'm only here for the gear"— as opposed to reverent imitation of tenkara as practiced in the mountains of Japan.

Japanese tenkara celebrities respond politely when asked about westerners' approach to tenkara.

"I think tenkara is about fishing in the beautiful mountain streams of Japan, for our beautiful native trout which inhabit them," the famed Masami Sakakibara, aka Tenkara no Oni, told Tenkara-Fisher.com. Once tenkara "enters another country and culture, people who pick up a tenkara rod there have the right and obligation to decide what tenkara is for them. It is certainly not for me to decide."

Others have said the same. Of course, Sakakibara, like Trow, Sment, Stewart, Galhardo, and the rest of the tenkara entrepreneurs, has a stake in widespread use of tenkara rods in the US. He sells a line of high-end tenkara rods. The more kinds of water and fish that are considered suitable for tenkara fishing, the better for the tenkara industry's business.

Adam Klagsbrun, on the other hand, has no financial stake in the tenkara business (though he did dabble in reselling some wet-wading gear years ago). A native New Yorker now living in Boulder, Colorado, Klags is an outspoken devotee of Japanese tenkara in all its aspects: remote streams, rugged terrain, light lines, light flies, wild trout, edible flora, campfires. He doesn't mind a bit if you want to use a heavy tenkara rod to catch pike or catfish, but he doesn't think you should call it tenkara. He does think you should try to learn the authentic Japanese approach, which is about more than just catching trout.

"If the goal is to catch fish, everyone should fish the way they want to," he said. "But they have no right to call that something that it isn't. They have no right to redefine through their ignorance something that exists."

Adam, who is thirty-five, grew up on New York's Upper West Side, in the building where part of the movie *Death Wish* was filmed. He got a fly rod for his bar mitzvah and learned to fly-fish in the small streams that flowed between the city's reservoirs in hilly Westchester County. I met him in New York, at meetings of the city chapter of Trout Unlimited in the Orvis store on Fifth Avenue. Not long after, he took half a year off and hiked the Pacific Crest and John Muir trails, tenkara fishing the whole way. He now lives in Boulder and works in the medical marijuana industry.

He discovered tenkara not long after it was introduced. "I really found it through ultralight backpacking," he said. "I don't have to carry the reel, I don't have to carry my rod tube, the whole bit. At first I was just fishing with it, like everyone else." He learned about using light level lines held off the water, and his tenkara knowledge grew more sophisticated.

Eventually he visited Japan, and quickly realized Japanese tenkara was different from what we were doing in the States. Many Americans were simply using their tenkara rods to fish the same way they used to with fly rods.

"That was the moment I realized just how wrong we have it here," he said. "Not for lack of Daniel [Galhardo] trying, because he told that story correctly when he got here. But that got overpowered, and he gave up. Everybody did."

As Adam sees it, the American tenkara companies that have sprung up over the past decade could have emphasized the Japanese approach, but didn't bother.

"It's probably because it's easier to sell rods; it's probably because it's easier to make everyone like you; but a lot of people decided they weren't going to care," he said.

"We have every company using misleading, factually incorrect marketing. To them, it's a marketing term that they can slap on a Chinese blank and sell."

On social media, Klags is outspoken and blunt on the subject of what should and shouldn't be considered tenkara. He's been called elitist, and doesn't argue that he's not. In this context, he sees elitism as a virtue—choosing a more difficult way to fish and getting good at it, because fishing is about more than just catching fish.

"Anyone with a tenkara rod is elitist," he said. "Anyone who's fly-fishing is elitist. Stop pretending elite is a negative term. . . . Tenkara doesn't need to grow. Tenkara doesn't need to be spread to every corner of the fly-fishing world. And tenkara is not for beginners. People who have certain goals, who want to catch fish in certain ways, that's who tenkara is for."

Of course, it's not unusual for a thing to evolve differently when it is transplanted somewhere else, whether it's food, art, or politics. Or, for that matter, baseball, as Badger Tenkara points out, which is played a little differently in Japan but it is still unmistakably baseball.

John Vetterli was among the first Americans to visit Japan to learn about real tenkara. A lifelong student of many aspects of Japanese culture, he was the first American member of the Harima Tenkara Club. He knows what tenkara looks like in Japan. But he is also one of the first Americans to use a tenkara rod to catch big carp in brown water under a highway overpass, just for the hell of it. He sees it as inevitable, and not especially regrettable, that tenkara would become Americanized.

"This is America. We're going to do what we're going to do, and nobody is going to change that," Vetterli said. "America has always bastardized other cultures to make things our own. It's the melting-pot thing."

And while some Japanese (typically younger tenkara zealots) lament the things Americans are doing and calling tenkara, others have a more live-and-let-live perspective, he said.

"When you talk to the old guys who've been doing it for forty years, they say, 'I don't care what you do as long as you're having fun, but respect the culture and the history,'" he said.

When Tenkara USA introduced its Hane rod model in 2018, the rod was posed on company's website next to a big bass, caught in Texas.

All along, Daniel Galhardo has drawn a distinction between tenkara, the gear, which can theoretically be used to catch almost anything, and tenkara, the method, the essence of which is simplicity.

"On the one hand, tenkara is this thing that's been around for a long time, practiced by a certain group of people in a certain environment for a certain kind of fish, and it has a certain look to it," he said. "On the other hand, you

John Vetterli learning tenkara from Hiromichi Fuji, one of the men who established modern recreational tenkara fishing in Japan. JOHN VETTERLI

have the tool, and it's a rod, line, and fly, and however you rig it is up to you. I've tried to be clear about the distinction from the very beginning. I have certainly been interested in sharing tenkara fishing the way it's done in Japan, not out of a sense of tradition so much as it's really a way to keep fly fishing simple.

"In my personal opinion, it never quite included fish species as a restriction," he said. "Tenkara has a certain essence to it, it has a feel to it, it looks a certain way, and it can have that essence if you're fishing for trout, if you're fishing for panfish, if you're fishing for bass. I think businesses and guides that are promoting tenkara have a responsibility to not make it more complicated than it needs to be."

ERiK Ostrander may speak for many of us when he says he's sensitive to tenkara's original meaning yet finds its definition expanding in the translation from Japan to the Western world.

"We don't know what to call it, but we're trying not to call it tenkara," ERiK said. "Tenkara is a very small description of fixed-line fly fishing. But in the US, it's not that. It's very big, and very broad. And I've always wanted to know all the things you can do with a tenkara rod."

CHAPTER 20

Q&A with Go Ishii

As Americans and Europeans work to better understand tenkara in Japan, the English-Japanese language barrier is a formidable obstacle. Tokyo resident Go Ishii has emerged as the foremost translator for the tenkara communities in both countries. The role requires more than fluency in both languages; Go is an expert angler who can convey the subtleties. He's also been generous with his time and his connections as westerners, most notably Paul Gaskell and John Pearson of Discover Tenkara, have come seeking knowledge.

You spent considerable time in the US. Where did you live and what did you do?

I didn't speak any English when I decided I wanted to go to school in the states at age twelve, and I was actually recommended a language school in Victoria, British Columbia. I spent three months there with a host family and it was great. I was young enough to pick up most daily conversation necessary in that time, and I was ready for real schooling in the US.

Through seventh and eighth grade, I went to a boarding school in Ojai, California. They took us on amazing outdoors adventures regularly, such as a seven-day trek through the Grand Canyon, sailboat adventures, trip to Yosemite, and more.

I wanted to see more of the country so I went to a prep school in Maine for high school, then tried out some city life in Boston, attending a university there for a few years. The big school in a big city didn't really work out for me so I took some time off and traveled through North America in a van for six months or so.

It's more than just fishing. Go Ishii at a tenkara camp in Japan. GO ISHII

Eventually, I ended up in Olympia, Washington, going back to school and started working in real estate. I decided to return to Japan when I was thirty to spend much-needed time with my aging mother, and I live in Tokyo now with my wife, Catherine.

When did you begin tenkara fishing? How did you first become aware of it?

I started fishing in the mountains of Japan near where I grew up, in Kanagawa prefecture, when I was nine or ten years old. It was bait fishing at first, and I started buying books and magazines on the subject. In one of the magazines, there was a picture of a man catching iwana with a tenkara rod and I became curious right away. It was very difficult casting under trees and into tight spots in the rapids at first. . . . Then I started going to school in the US and could only fish in Japan during summer breaks so it actually took me a long time to catch my first trout with tenkara. I think I was seventeen or eighteen when it happened. Since then, I only fish tenkara when fishing in the mountains but I do other kinds of fishing such as saltwater lure fishing, too, to mix things up.

Do you also have experience with Western-style fly fishing? How does it relate to tenkara fishing?

Many of the friends I have in both the US and Japan are great fly fishermen, and I've tried it here and there. I've fished for stripers off the coast of Cape Cod, had some great trout-fishing experiences in Montana, and a little bit in Japan as well. There are many ways to compare fly fishing to tenkara, but I might say it's like the difference between shooting with a rifle and a handgun. You're doing the same thing but with different tools and techniques. They're designed to serve different purposes and, quite frankly, I think they're both equally fun. It's just that tenkara is perhaps more ideal for fish in the mountain streams of Japan than the Western rig.

Can you give us any sense of how prevalent fly fishing and tenkara fishing are in Japan, and how prevalent they are compared to one another? Is there an "us vs. them" quality to the relationship between the two disciplines, as there sometimes is in the US?

When Japan opened its ports to the outside in mid-1800s, many foreign diplomats, engineers, scientists, and merchants came from European countries. Many of them brought their fly-fishing rods, and even brought their own trout species such as brook and rainbow trout. So fly fishing has been around some time here, and it really picked up after the war. I think the concept of gamefishing was cool and fashionable, maybe refreshing to a nation where most of fishing done at the time was for consumption. Companies like TIEMCO [TMC] and C&F Design are some of the companies that grew to internationally recognized fly-fishing brands out of Japan and there are many more.

Today, it seems general cost of fly fishing is driving some of the people away from it, and, on the other hand, tenkara is gaining more popularity than ever before. I do sense the "us vs. them" sometimes with bait anglers and everyone else, but not so much between fly fishermen and tenkara anglers in Japan. Since most of the fly fishermen also fish in the mountains, there's a lot we can relate to. We're all there to appreciate the beautiful mountains, streams, and our pretty char or trout species after all.

Go Ishii and backcountry tenkara pioneer Yuzo Sebata examining a couple of Sebata's prized handmade lines. GO ISHII

Certain ideas about tenkara took hold in the US in the years after it was introduced: that Japanese anglers only use one fly; that almost all trout caught in Japan are small; that level-line, tight-line fishing is the only true method. We have learned in recent years that the picture is more complicated. Thoughts?
Well, the fish-size issue is true to some extent in the mountains. In lakes and in lower sections of rivers, we've seen world-record trout caught multiple times, but not with tenkara. In Japan, we have a lot of amazing mountain streams, but we also have a lot of anglers. I've heard some three million people visit the mountain streams in Japan annually and a good percentage of them still catch and kill. In a lot of places, we

just don't have any large fish left. You have to either fish in less attractive places such as way downstream closer to civilization, or go way deep away from trails and get to places others won't (which is actually fun) to catch good-size fish constantly.

The fly or the rig you use is your style and whatever suits the angler is fine, I think. But if you want to come to Japan and catch some of our ultra-skittish fish in the mountains, you have to be able to cast a light line and get the fly in that very small spot or short lane. I recommend light level lines because they get the job done, and you can buy a 200-meter spool of it for around twenty dollars. These lines I'm talking about are not being sold as tenkara lines, but are either fluoro carbon or stiff nylon lines, and completely sufficient. Too many brands now target new tenkara anglers and charge more for less, especially for lines, and a lot of my friends and myself try to avoid them.

Your perfect English and your willingness to act as a facilitator for American visitors and journalists has made you a very important interpreter of tenkara to the Western world. Do you enjoy this role? How do Japanese tenkara anglers feel about the way tenkara has caught on in America?

Well, to be completely honest, I would not have met so many tenkara anglers from all over Japan and the world had I not put myself in that position, and I'm quite thankful for how it turned out. People are always introducing me to more people, and the challenge these days for me is trying to stay connected with them all. It's a lot of socializing and can actually be very time consuming. So I sit down with other anglers all the time and discuss over drinks about the way tenkara in America is catching on. But most of the time, I don't think they care so much as long as tenkara is done and passed on here in Japan as it has been for many generations.

Why do Japanese tenkara anglers prefer tenkara to fly fishing with a rod and reel? Especially the men who pioneered recreational tenkara fishing in the twentieth century. What was the appeal of fixed-line fishing? Tradition? Challenge? Tactical advantages?

Generally speaking, people say we need five items to fish: rod, line, weight, hook, and bait. With tenkara, you only need three: rod, line, and *kebari* (fly).

I think myself and many others prefer tenkara when fishing in the mountains because the simplicity of it allows you to focus on other things.

When we enter the mountains, we don't just fish. There's usually a great deal of planning that goes in, since we visit different parts of Japan, chasing better waters and fish at different times of the year.

Many of us train during off-season to keep our legs strong for the coming season. The physical challenge of it, too, such as trekking with a heavy pack and climbing, or swimming through ice cold water, is tough but quite satisfying.

There's a lot of thought that goes into gear, and I'm not talking about just fishing gear, but gear to ensure our safety in the mountains and to maximize the experience.

My typical tenkara trip goes something like this.

1) Spend anywhere between a week to a few months planning a trip, depending on the seriousness of the destination environment.
2) Friday after work, drive four-plus hours to the destination, which is usually the end of a dirt road, where the trail begins. Spend the night there.
3) Get up early and hit the trail. Hike anywhere between one and four hours.
4) Reach camp site and set up base camp.
5) Fish and trek upstream. We only make a few casts to a spot then move upstream, so if we fish quickly, we often cover a few miles of river on one fishing outing.
6) While fishing or trekking, look for edible plants or mushrooms and harvest for dinner.
7) Build a fire at camp site, cook, and most importantly drink. We can chill our

drinks in rivers since they stay very cold year around. There's nothing like being out in the elements and drinking up, talking about the day with people you share your passion with. I do not recommend drinking on solo trips since you need to be on your toes the whole time out there.

8) With all the effort of getting there, it's best to spend a few nights there, and explore more upstream.

9) Trek back to the car, go for a dip in a hot spring, and look for something good and local to eat.

10) Go home.

You may notice that the fishing aspect of it is really only a fraction of the experience. It's the full package. I'm not sure if there's an activity or experience that is more fulfilling than fishing in the mountains, and it doesn't have to be tenkara. Many fly fishermen and spin-rod anglers I know fish the same way. But the light and simple gear of tenkara is very attractive to those who want to minimize the weight and volume. You can practice and acquire most skills needed for tenkara in several years if you're committed, I think, but if you added the fun and challenge of mountaineering or foraging, it really becomes a lifelong passion.

CHAPTER 21

Tenkara Flies

You can cast any fly you like with a tenkara rod. You can use what have become thought of as tenkara flies, which are discussed in this chapter. But you can also use your tenkara rod to fish regular American flies like the Adams or the Gold-Ribbed Hare's Ear (or the Royal Coachman Wet, like Ed Van Put).

There is, however, a philosophical difference between American (and Japanese) fly fishers and Japanese tenkara fishing. While it may have been overplayed in the early translation of tenkara from Japan to the West, Japanese tenkara experts enjoy limiting themselves to a small selection of simple, basic flies and relying on their stalking and casting skills to catch trout, rather than having the "right fly" tied to their lines.

Having lots of different flies, and knowing exactly when to use each one, has been an essential part of Western fly fishing for centuries. It goes back to *The Treatyse of Fysshynge Wyth an Angle*, published in 1496, widely thought to be the first book about fly fishing, in which the author describes twelve flies you need to catch trout.

Anglers of the day could have probably dreamed up twelve more that were just as good, and could also probably have picked their favorite three and caught plenty of trout. But the *Treatyse*, with its nice round number (months of the year?), established the importance of having an assortment of flies.

In the early years, we Americans were told there were Japanese tenkara anglers who used one fly and one fly only, no matter what real insects the fish were feeding on. It turns out that there were very few anglers in Japan who so restricted

---

Tenkara flies are whimsical, utilitarian, beautiful. and effective. MORGAN LYLE

Sculptor Matt Hart's statue of a tenkara fly on display at the Catskill Fly Fishing Center and Museum in 2018. MORGAN LYLE

themselves. They may not have had a half-dozen copies for every life stage of every insect that could possibly be found in their local streams, as some Western fly fishers aspire to do, but the Japanese do enjoy making and using different kinds of flies. Part of the fun of fly fishing, with a fly rod or a tenkara rod, is knowing about patterns and choosing the one that seems best for the conditions.

Even so, it is an accepted principle both in the US and Japan that fly pattern doesn't matter all that much in some situations. One of those situations is a small, rushing mountain stream, where aquatic insects aren't as abundant as they are on large, calmer rivers. This is the kind of water where tenkara evolved. Trout in such streams aren't very choosy about flies.

A general, impressionistic fly pattern of a reasonable size will generally take trout in such situations, especially if it is cast so that it lands lightly and drifts naturally, and the fish can't see the angler.

On the other hand, if you find yourself waist-deep in a wide, flat, slow-moving pool on the Delaware River along the New York–Pennsylvania border, with trout rising all around you, you may need to choose your fly very carefully indeed. In a relatively stable and consistently coldwater environment like that, specific kinds of mayflies hatch in very large numbers every day for weeks at a time. The trout get used to eating the same bug all day long. If they're eating size 20 Sulfur mayflies, whose bodies are smaller than a grain of rice, a size 12 Sakasa *Kebari* probably won't even register as possible food.

Your choices in that situation would be to use a Western-style fly of the right size, say a tiny orange-yellow Compara-dun dry fly, or go someplace with stony water and rushing currents.

A New Style of Fly

English-speaking fly fishers have a lot of magazines, websites, and books on flies and fly tying at their disposal. I wrote one myself. The Japanese have plenty of published material, too, but most of us can't read it; the last census reported fewer than half a million Americans speak Japanese at home. The American tenkara community has relied on a single Japanese website written in English to teach us about the flies catching trout in the mountains of Japan.

Trout and Seasons of the Mountain Village—"My Best Streams" was first posted in 1997 by a man named Yoshikazu Fujioka. As its name suggests, much of it describes Japanese trout streams and regions, and has been updated to include Fujioka's recent fishing trips to the States. But the site is also the Rosetta Stone of Japanese tenkara flies, with photos of dozens of patterns, complete with informative captions about who invented them and how they are used.

Unlike Western fly tiers, going all the way back to the *Treatyse*, the Japanese seldom, if ever, give their flies names. A fly is usually referred to by the name of the person who invented it or the place where they fished.

The first time a Japanese expert gave a public fly-tying demonstration in America was in May 2009, when Hisao Ishigaki gave a talk on tenkara at the Catskill Fly Fishing Center and Museum in Livingston Manor, New York.

Translated by Misako Ishimura, coauthor of *Tenkara: Radically Simple, Ultralight Fly-Fishing*, and surrounded by historical memorabilia from famous American fly fishers, Ishigaki explained the tenkara angler's view of what makes a fish bite—a significantly different approach from American and European fly fishing.

Ishigaki then sat down at a fly-tying vise and made a *kebari*, the Japanese word for trout fly, which I've seen translated as "feather-needle." The fly he made is his signature pattern and has come to be called the Ishigaki Kebari by the American tenkara community. It looks considerably different from what most American anglers are accustomed to.

Most striking was how little Ishigaki included in his fly. It consisted of a slender thread body and a propeller of rooster hackle feather just

It's nothing more than a hook, a rooster feather, and a few inches of thread, but the Ishigaki Kebari is a brilliant example of minimalism in fly design.
MORGAN LYLE

behind the eye of the hook. Body and hackle are two crucial elements of a great many Western trout flies but most of them have more: a tail, fur "dubbed" onto the thread for a plumper body, wings made of feather tips or animal hairs, perhaps a "rib" spiraled up the body.

American fly tiers (like me) often have Tupperware boxes full of carefully selected threads and furs and expensive skins from roosters genetically bred to have specific colors and consistencies. Ishigaki used department-store black thread and a run-of-the-mill brown feather for his fly, and declared it ready to catch trout.

The fly had a very different look from American or European flies. It was meant to be used as a wet fly, meaning it is fished below the surface of the water, as opposed to a dry fly, which is designed to float on the surface. Western wet flies are almost always tied with the barbs of the hackle feather leaning rearward, toward the bend of the hook. This gives the impression of a swimming or drifting aquatic insect whose legs are trailing as they dangle from its body. On Ishigaki's fly, the hackle feather fibers leaned forward, over the eye of the fly.

I have read that this design is more a matter of tradition than strategic advantage. But it is true that hackle leaning forward remains more visible than rearward hackle, because it doesn't collapse along the body when the fly is tugged through the water. The fibers do bend backward a bit when the fly is tugged, but then spring forward again between tugs, providing motion that seems to convey the impression of a live, struggling insect.

Forward-leaning hackles, especially if they are stiff, can also prevent a fly from slipping through the water too easily. This is useful when "manipulating" or jigging a wet fly to entice

trout to strike. You need the fly to hold its position even while hopping up and down; with no hackle helping to anchor it, the fly might slide too far toward the angler or even pop out of the water altogether.

The fly Ishigaki showed us was built differently from most Western flies. If you tie, you will find this interesting. The typical Western fly is constructed from the back of the hook to the front; more precisely, it starts at the bend of the hook and is finished just behind the eye. The last thing tied on a Western fly is its "head," a smooth ball of thread at the very front end; the knot used to lock the head in place is usually the only one on the whole fly. Making the head was one of the first things Ishigaki did, and the knot that

This Copper and Grouse Sakasa Kebari, tied by Anthony Naples of Three Rivers Tenkara, is a great example of the *sakasa*, or reverse, hackle. Leaning out over the eye of the hook rather than back toward the bend, the feather tips move in a lifelike way in the water. MORGAN LYLE

The Mop Fly is hardly a classic tenkara pattern, and it's a little clunky to cast, but it catches fish. MORGAN LYLE

held the whole fly together was made at the bend of the hook instead of behind the eye. He tied on the feather, created the head, wrapped the feather around the hook to splay its fibers, then made the body as the last step in making the fly.

Ishigaki's demonstration was the beginning of a new school of fly tying in the United States. The simplicity of his fly and its unique (to us) construction have been adopted and adapted by American fly tiers.

But as information about tenkara made its way across the Pacific, we soon learned that the Ishigaki Kebari was just one of many Japanese-style trout flies. And many of them were very different from the fly Ishigaki tied that day in the Catskills.

It turned out that most Japanese wet flies have hackle that leans rearward, just like those in the West. The *sakasa*, or reverse, style is in the minority. Some don't lean in either direction but stick out perpendicular to the body, like Western-style dry flies. (The rearward-leaning style is called *jun* and the stiff perpendicular hackle is called *futsuu*.)

Lots of Japanese flies have bodies made not of simple thread but of dubbing, peacock-tail feather fibers ("herls"), pheasant tail feather barbs, yarn, floss, and other materials found in Western fly tiers' Tupperware boxes.

Some Japanese tenkara flies have tails, wings, and ribs. Some are fairly elaborate. Some have hackles tied both in the front and at the back. Some Japanese anglers fish flies with metal bead heads, which help the fly sink and give it some flash but aren't considered classic tenkara.

Some Japanese flies are in fact meant to be imitations of specific caddisflies or mayflies, just like in the West.

Classical tenkara fishing employs flies meant to suggest aquatic insects, but streamer-style flies, designed to look like bait fish, are useful for trout and most other kinds of fish. The Soft-Hackle Streamer is extremely lightweight and casts nicely on a tenkara rod. MORGAN LYLE

In short, there's a wide variety of trout fly patterns made and used by Japanese tenkara anglers.

That being said, there is a general understanding of what constitutes a tenkara fly in America. Over here, it's likely to have a simple body and a *sakasa* hackle, and probably doesn't have a tail or wings. Many American fly fishers find it important to match natural flies even if that means using really tiny imitations, and some tenkara anglers do, too. But the tenkara tradition is to use flies around size 12, or about a half-inch long.

In Japan, as in the United States and Europe and anywhere people fly fish, making one's own flies is an involved and absorbing hobby in its own right. There is a special satisfaction in catching a fish on a lure you made yourself.

There are many good books on how to tie flies. I like to think my own book, *Simple Flies: 52 Easy-to-Tie Flies That Catch Fish*, is one of them. There are helpful videos galore on the Internet. Chris Stewart's own exquisite tying videos sometimes pop up in searches. And no one who is interested in fly tying should fail to watch the excellent Tightlines Productions fly-tying videos.

Following is a small selection of tenkara flies, Western flies that have been adopted by the tenkara community, or my personal favorites. You can make them yourself, and most of them are also available for sale by any number of commercial fly tiers.

TAKAYAMA KEBARI

ISHIGAKI KEBARI

Like most Japanese flies, this beautiful pattern is named after the place it was commonly used—in this case, the city of Takayama in the mountainous Gifu prefecture in the central part of the country. Again, colors are up to the fly tier, but the red body is a classic design. Feel free to substitute brown or gray partridge hackle if you like.

- **Hook:** #16-10 Daiichi 1130 or similar wet fly hook
- **Hackle:** Hen pheasant
- **Thread:** Red
- **Body:** Tying thread
- **Collar:** Peacock herl

Made of nothing but a black thread body and a brown hackle, this slender fly has become the embodiment of tenkara's disciplined simplicity. Ishigaki's two versions were black/brown and gray/grizzly, but you can make them any colors you want. Yellow/cream, all black, and all cream are worth a try.

- **Hook:** #16-12 straight-shanked dry fly or wet fly
- **Hackle:** Rooster hackle for dry flies, brown or grizzly
- **Thread:** Black or gray 140-denier fly-tying thread, or sewing thread

AKIYAMAGO KEBARI

The brilliant Discover Tenkara team did much to publicize this very cool fly, which was first published on "My Best Streams." It's yet another pattern that can be customized and adapted to the tier's needs.

- **Hook:** Owner Keiryu hook, Japanese #4 (approx. #12 Western)
- **Hackle:** Dry fly, color to suit tier, palmered over entire shank, trimmed on rear two-thirds
- **Tag:** Red Floss
- **Thread:** 140- or 70-denier, color to suit tier

ROBB CHUNCO'S FUTSUU KEBARI

A fine example of the futsuu style, which many Western fly fishers will think of as a dry fly, due to its stiff rooster hackle. It is in fact meant to be fished underwater, but like many tenkara flies can be floated on the surface instead if you suspect the fish are "looking up."

- **Hook:** #14 Firehole Stick 633
- **Hackle:** Dark barred ginger
- **Body:** Yellow embroidery thread
- **Tag:** Red UNI thread

KILLER BUG

KEEPER KEBARI

Invented by Englishman Frank Sawyer, this brilliant nymph was publicized by Tenkara Bum Chris Stewart and adopted early on by the American tenkara community. The original color is best, but black, brown, olive, purple, or any other color of Jamieson's Shetland Spindrift can also be effective. Add a bead if you want weight and flash. Add a hackle and it becomes Stewart's Killer Kebari.

- **Hook:** #12 Fulling Mill Heavyweight Champ
- **Underbody:** Fine copper wire (add a drop of superglue)
- **Body:** Jamieson's Shetland Spindrift yarn in oyster

Chris Stewart made a large Killer Bug out of black yarn, gave it a rib and a hackle and began using it to catch fat bass on his annual trips to Maine. It also strikes me as a good stonefly imitation for trout fishing.

- **Hook:** #6-8 Daiichi 1560
- **Underbody:** Fine copper wire (add a drop of superglue)
- **Body:** Jamieson's Shetland Spindrift yarn in black

KILLER BUGGER

COPPER AND GROUSE SAKASA KEBARI

Another member of the Killer Bug family, this fly is a take on the classic Woolly Bugger. It reportedly caught fifty-four species of fish during a TenkaraBum.com contest in 2014. It is said to be effective as tiny as size 20, but I think of this as a big fly and tie and fish it in sizes 12 to 6.

- **Hook:** #12-6 Daiichi 1560
- **Underbody:** Fine copper wire (add a drop of superglue)
- **Body:** Jamieson's Shetland Spindrift yarn in black
- **Tail:** Black marabou

This fly was introduced by Anthony Naples of Three Rivers Tenkara in Pittsburgh. Its wire body gives it shine and weight, its grouse hackle gives it wiggly legs, and the peacock herl collar recalls the Takayama kebari. It should work on everything from brook trout to Atlantic salmon.

- **Hook:** #12 Mustad 3906B, 3X heavy, 2X long
- **Hackle:** Grouse covert
- **Body:** Heavy copper wire
- **Collar:** Peacock herl
- **Thread:** Hot red 70- or 140-denier

DEER HAIR EMERGER

DEER HAIR CADDIS DRY FLY

Designed by Bob Wyatt of New Zealand, this fly had an enormous impact on my fishing. These days, it's pretty much the only floating fly I use. Actually, the wing floats, but the abdomen hangs down below the surface, and that's the key to the fly's success.

- **Hook:** #12-16 Daiichi 1155 or similar curved-shank hook
- **Wing:** Deer hair
- **Body:** Hare's mask dubbing
- **Thread:** Brown 140-denier

A sibling of the Deer Hair Emerger, the Deer Hair Caddis is a basic down-wing fly that catches fish feeding on caddis and even mayflies.

- **Hook:** #10-18 standard dry fly
- **Wing:** Deer hair
- **Body:** Hare's mask dubbing
- **Thread:** Tan 140-denier (70-denier for smaller flies)

ROYAL COACHMAN WET

MOP FLY

This is the fly that Ed Van Put used with so much success with his Japanese mountain stream rod. It's been catching trout for many generations.

- **Hook:** Standard wet fly, 1XL
- **Wing:** White goose wing quill section
- **Body:** Peacock herl with red floss band
- **Tail:** Golden pheasant crest
- **Hackle:** Brown hen
- **Thread:** Black 140- or 70-denier

It's a finger of spongy microfiber clipped off a bath mat or car duster, tied to a hook. Fly-tying art, it is not. The Mop Fly emerged from the competition circuit, and it's a great trout fly. (I caught a small northern pike on one, too, in hot orange.) Adding a collar of dubbing might make you feel more like you've actually tied a fly, but will make no difference to the fish.

- **Hook:** #8-10 nymph hook, 1X heavy
- **Body:** Microfiber finger from duster
- **Bead:** ⅛-inch Tungsten, tier's choice of color
- **Collar:** Dubbing, tier's choice of color
- **Thread:** Tan 140-denier, tier's choice of color

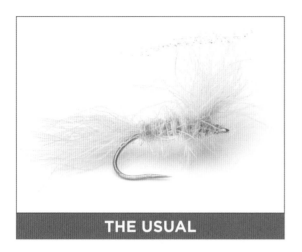

THE USUAL

GARTSIDE SOFT HACKLE STREAMER

This shaggy blob of a dry fly has been catching trout since its birth in the Adirondack Mountains of New York in the mid-twentieth century. It has an upright wing and a tail, so it's generally thought of as a mayfly imitation. It's easy to see in the low light of evening, and trout do seem to like it a lot.

- **Hook:** #10-14 dry fly
- **Body:** Snowshoe hare's foot fur
- **Wing:** Snowshoe hare's foot fur
- **Tail:** Snowshoe hare's foot fur
- **Thread:** Hot orange, 140- or 70-denier

This is the lightest streamer fly I know, which makes it good for tenkara casting, but it's on this list because it's a very effective fly. Made of marabou feather, it moves and quivers in the water, giving the strong impression of a living thing. It can be tied in any color.

- **Hook:** #6 Daiichi 1560 nymph or similar
- **Wing:** 1 blood marabou feather
- **Collar:** Mallard flank or other soft, long-fibered feather, tier's choice of color
- **Flash:** 3-6 strands of Krystal Flash
- **Thread:** Tier's choice of color, 70- or 140-denier

Further Reading and Resources

Explaining tenkara and telling its history to the Western audience was challenging, due to the language barrier. Retailers, authors, and journalists dug in, often sourcing their reporting straight from the Japanese masters themselves. These are among the resources I have relied on the most in my own tenkara education.

TenkaraUSA.com

In order to sell tenkara rods, Daniel Galhardo had to first explain how and why to use them. Tenkara USA's website is a repository of education and storytelling, with lots of great videos and illustrations. Galhardo is also the author of a book, *Tenkara: The Book*, featuring instruction and personal anecdotes, told in an encouraging and upbeat voice.

TenkaraBum.com

Chris Stewart's website is a charming, eloquent, and candid treatment of tenkara gear and technique. His descriptions of the rods he sells are the most comprehensive and detailed in the tenkara industry. He sells much more than rods, and all of the gear gets the same serious coverage.

Discover Tenkara

Paul Gaskell and John Pearson are also retailers but, apart from a small line of high-end rods, they don't sell gear—they sell knowledge. They made multiple trips to Japan to interview the tenkara masters, and have unearthed tenkara's history in unparalleled detail. Their videos and e-books are top quality, and they made a great deal of excellent content available for free on their YouTube series, *Tenkara in Focus*.

Teton Tenkara

Tom Davis has nothing to sell. He simply shares his experiences with tenkara rods and gear while fishing small, secluded creeks in Idaho for wild cutthroat trout. In the process, he passes along impartial reviews in meticulous detail. The blog is informative, enjoyable, and an invaluable resource for anyone researching tenkara rods in advance of making a purchase.

Tenkara Talk

The best-known blog on tenkara and one of the first, Jason Klass's Tenkara Talk, has been one of the most important venues for information on the sport. Jason was already a veteran fly fisherman and guide when he discovered tenkara in 2009, and his angling background informed his exploration of tenkara, to his readers' benefit. Tenkara Talk is the first place I go when researching a tenkara topic.

Tenkara Fisher

Adam Trahan was a very early adopter of tenkara and has been one of its premier scholars for a decade. Trahan has interviewed dozens of Japanese tenkara masters, and his blog is a treasure trove of information in the masters' own words. Tenkara Fisher is an incredible resource, and Trahan has done more than anyone to bridge the Pacific and share authentic tenkara knowledge with the Western world.

Tenkara Angler Magazine

The only magazine devoted entirely to tenkara, the quarterly *Tenkara Angler*, is available for free online or in a handsome print version for twenty-five dollars. Each issue offers a diverse range of articles from the most prominent authorities on the sport, and new voices are represented as well.

Tenkara: Radically Simple, Ultralight Fly Fishing

Published by Lyons Press in 2011, this book by Dr. Kevin Kelleher and Misako Ishimura is the first book about tenkara in English. It was many Americans' first introduction to tenkara.

Tenkara Fly Fishing: Insights and Strategies

New York outdoor writer and multimedia content producer David E. Dirks compiled the experiences and collective wisdom of many of the country's top tenkara experts (and also me) in this comprehensive book.

Simple Fly Fishing: Techniques for Tenkara and Rod & Reel

Patagonia founder Yvon Chouinard is the most famous person to embrace tenkara. His book, coauthored by Craig Mathews and Mauro Mazzo and beautifully illustrated by the renowned James Prosek, did much to elevate tenkara's stature.

Index

Note: Page numbers in *italics* indicate/include photo captions.

SINCE TENKARA WAS INTRODUCED to the United States in 2009, it has become a rapidly growing trend and many anglers have adapted the traditional Japanese techniques for waters in the United States. This comprehensive book covers the current state of tenkara—the best flies, the equipment, and essential techniques. It also tells the stories of the people who brought tenkara to America and examines this Eastern method's place in the Western sport-fishing world. Non-anglers and experts alike will find it fascinating, informative, and fun.

MORGAN LYLE is the author of *Simple Flies: 52 Easy-to-Tie Patterns That Catch Fish*. He has written dozens of articles for *American Angler*, *Fly Tyer*, *The Drake*, *Trout*, and other magazines, and his writing has appeared in the *New York Times* and *Newsday*. Morgan has written the "On the Fly" column for the *New York Outdoor News* since the paper's inception in 2004 and serves as the master of ceremonies for the Catskill Fly Fishing Center and Museum Hall of Fame induction ceremony. Morgan does most of his fishing in fresh and saltwater in New York, Massachusetts, and Connecticut. He lives in Brooklyn, New York.

Photos by George Daniel
Cover illustration © Nastasic/Getty Images
Cover design by Amanda Wilson

STACKPOLE BOOKS

An imprint of
The Rowman & Littlefield Publishing Group, Inc.
StackpoleBooks.com

Distributed by NATIONAL BOOK NETWORK
800-462-6420

$24.95 US
ISBN 978-0-8117-3782-1

52495

9 780811 737821